Inv 10
(26)

£2·50

Summon's
CHRISTIAN
MISCELLANY

FOR HEATHER, GRACE AND FAITH

Summon's CHRISTIAN MISCELLANY

Parminder Summon

A LION BOOK

Copyright © 2004 Parminder Summon

The author asserts the moral right
to be identified as the author of this work

A Lion Book
an imprint of
Lion Hudson plc
Mayfield House, 256 Banbury Road,
Oxford OX2 7DH, England
www.lionhudson.com
ISBN 0 7459 5174 0

First edition 2004
10 9 8 7 6 5 4 3 2 1 0

A catalogue record for this book is available
from the British Library

Typeset in 11/12 Venetian 301
Printed and bound in Finland

Parminder Singh Summon was born in India, 445 years after Martin Luther marched along to the Castle Church in Wittenberg with his 95 Theses. Three years later, the Holy Roman Emperor, Charles V, excommunicated him (Martin Luther, that is). Parminder attended Crocketts Lane Infant School, Parkside Junior School, Thomas Telford High School and West Park College in Birmingham. Later on, he gained a degree and then another degree.

He works for Cancer Research UK and he worships with Nene Family Church in Peterborough, UK. He has worked as a Government policy adviser and as a business adviser in the field of economic development. He is an avid collector of trifles and a trifling collector of avids. He has written on the tedious subject of the economic impact of Small and Medium Sized Enterprises (SMEs).

Parminder Summon has been a Christian for over 20 years and, in his spare time, he helps Gideons International with their work. Two of his greatest wishes (aside from world peace and an end to hunger) are to be the best man at a wedding and to be a godfather.

FOUR CLASSES OF MEN

He who knows not, and knows not he knows not –
shun him for he is a fool
He who knows not, and knows he knows not –
teach him for he is simple
He who knows, and knows not he knows –
wake him up for he is asleep
He who knows and knows he knows –
follow him for he is wise.
Arabic proverb

Summon's Christian Miscellany is a collection of things you didn't know you didn't know; a multilayered cornucopia of fascinating facts that enables you to peek at the diversity of a transforming faith. Christianity throws up so many issues and questions – this is an attempt to consider a few. *Summon's Christian Miscellany* – a useful reference source for quiz compilers, a great way to expand your knowledge and a compelling diversion into the narrow byways of the world's most popular religion (more than two billion adherents). Look here if you want to find out about:

Unusual Patron Saints

Ten Commandments for the Road

Christmas Carol Origins

Seven Deadly Sins and Seven Heavenly Virtues

The Origins of Basketball

Strange Bible Versions

The Alpha Course

Urim and Thummim

The Most Popular Verse in the Bible in Various Languages

The Top 10 Longest and Shortest Papal Reigns

Classes of Angels

Christian Music Festivals

Calvinism

Martin Luther

Patron Saints of Football Clubs

Clerical Vestments

Augustus Toplady

The Names of Jesus

How to Calculate the Date for Easter

Immovable Feasts of the Russian Orthodox Church

William Carey

The Christian Vegetarian Association

The Puritans

St Patrick's Lorica

Bible Translations into English

The Cambridge Seven

The Narnia Books by C.S. Lewis

Christian Nobel Laureates

> And this is my prayer: that your love may abound more and more
> in knowledge and depth of insight, so that you may be able to
> discern what is best and may be pure and blameless until the day
> of Christ, filled with the fruit of righteousness that comes
> through Jesus Christ – to the glory and praise of God.
> *Philippians* 1:9

WHEN YOU BURY A MAD DOG

Every effort has been made to ensure the information provided in this book is reliable. However, given the scope of the book, it is impossible to guarantee freedom from errors.

For errors, omissions, confusions and inelegant grammar (but no apostrophe pedants please), accept my apologies.

If you have ideas for suitable topics for future editions, improvements or amendments, please contact me care of Lion Hudson plc, Oxford, England, or via www.miscellany.info

> Forgive and forget. When you bury a mad dog,
> don't leave its tail above the ground.
> *Charles Haddon Spurgeon*

JOHN 3:16 IN VARIOUS LANGUAGES

ENGLISH
For God so loved the world that he gave his one and only Son, that whoever believes in him shall not perish but have eternal life.

AFRIKAANS
Want so lief het God die wêreld gehad, dat Hy sy eniggebore Seun gegee het, sodat elkeen wat in Hom glo, nie verlore mag gaan nie, maar die ewige lewe kan hê.

DANISH
Thi således elskede Gud verden, at han gav sin Søn den enbårne, for at enhver, som tror på ham, ikke skal fortabes, men have evigt liv.

FINNISH
Sillä niin on Jumala maailmaa rakastanut, että hän antoi ainokaisen Poikansa, ettei yksikään, joka häneen uskoo, hukkuisi, vaan hänellä olisi iankaikkinen elämä.

FRENCH
Car Dieu a tant aimé le monde qu'il a donné son Fils unique, afin que quiconque croit en lui ne périsse point, mais qu'il ait la vie éternelle.

GERMAN
Denn also hat Gott die Welt geliebt, daß er seinen eingebornen Sohn gab, auf daß alle, die an ihn glauben, nicht verloren werden, sondern das ewige Leben haben.

ITALIAN
Dio infatti ha tanto amato il mondo da dare il suo Figlio unigenito, perché chiunque crede in lui non muoia, ma abbia la vita eterna.

PORTUGUESE
Porque Deus amou o mundo de tal maneira, que deu o seu Filho unigênito, para que todo aquêle que nêle crê não pereça, mas tenha a vida eterna.

SPANISH
Porque de tal manera Amó Dios al mundo, que ha dado a su Hijo unigénito, para que todo aquel que en él cree no se pierda, mas tenga vida eterna.

SWEDISH
Ty så älskade Gud världen, att han utgav sin enfödde Son, på det att var och en som tror på honom skall icke förgås, utan hava evigt liv.

WELSH
Canys felly y carodd Duw y byd, fel y rhoddodd efe ei unig-anedig Fab, fel na choller pwy bynnag a gredo ynddo ef, ond caffael ohono fywyd tragwyddol.

TEN COMMANDMENTS FOR THE ROAD FROM THE CHRISTIAN ROAD SAFETY ASSOCIATION

1. Begin with a prayer.

2. If you start late, arrive late.

3. Alcohol is for the radiator, not the operator.

4. If entry into the flow of traffic is facilitated by the courtesy of another driver, wave in appreciation.

5. If you have inadvertently endangered the safe passage of another vehicle, wave as an apology.

6. Make it easy for aggressive opportunity snatchers to get ahead of you – far ahead.

7. Drive so that the sudden appearance of a police patrol car is a pleasant sight.

8. Give plenty of space to cars marked with dents.

9. Never accelerate, and decelerate if advisable, when another car wishes to enter your lane.

10. End every trip with a prayer of thanksgiving.

SIR CLIFF RICHARD

Born: 14 October 1940 in Lucknow, India

First performance: 14 July 1956 with The Quintones

Name change: April 1958 from Harry Webb to Cliff Richard

First recording session: July 1958 – Cliff Richard and The Drifters (who later renamed themselves The Shadows)

First number-one single: July 1959 – 'Move It': 'Living Doll'

First number-one album: October 1961 – *21 Today*

Conversion to Christianity: 26 June 1966

Summary of recording career:

Chart	Weeks on chart
Singles chart	1157
Album chart	808
Video chart	515
EP chart	432

Singles	Hits	No. Is	Albums	Hits	No. Is
1950s	6	2	1950s	2	0
1960s	43	7	1960s	22	3
1970s	22	I	1970s	10	I
1980s	31	2	1980s	11	2
1990s	20	2	1990s	8	I
2000s	3	–	2000s	3	0
Total	125	14	Total	56	7

Cliff's total worldwide sales now exceed 260 million.

THE BIBLE AND SHAKESPEARE

PHILIPPIANS 2:15
That ye may be blameless, and pure, & the sonnes of God without rebuke in the middes of a naughtie and crooked nation, among whome ye shine as lights in the world.
Geneva Bible

THE MERCHANT OF VENICE
Act 5, Scene 1 (61–2)
How far that little candle throws his beam!
So shines a good deed in a naughty world.

ROMANS 7:20
Now if I do what I do not want to do, it is no longer I who do it, but it is sin living in me that does it.

HAMLET
Act 5, Scene 2 (245–50)
Hamlet: If Hamlet from himself be ta'en away,
And when he's not himself does wrong Laertes,
Then Hamlet does it not, Hamlet denies it.
Who does it, then? His madness: if't be so,
Hamlet is of the faction that is wrong'd;
His madness is poor Hamlet's enemy.

EZEKIEL 34:15–16
I myself will tend my sheep and make them lie down, declares the Sovereign Lord. I will search for the lost and bring back the strays. I will bind up the injured and strengthen the weak, but the sleek and the strong I will destroy. I will shepherd the flock with justice.

TWO GENTLEMEN OF VERONA
Act 1, Scene 1 (73–81)
Proteus: Indeed, a sheep doth very often stray,
An if the shepherd be a while away.
Speed: You conclude that my master is a shepherd, then, and I a sheep?
Proteus: I do.
Speed: Why then, my horns are his horns, whether I wake or sleep.
Proteus: A silly answer and fitting well a sheep.

LUKE 18:25
Indeed, it is easier for a camel to go through the eye of a needle than for a rich man to enter the kingdom of God.

RICHARD II
Act 5, Scene 5 (17–18)
It is as hard to come as for a camel
To thread the postern of a small needle's eye.

SHOPPERS FOR CHRIST

Christians are not immune to consumerism and many products have been developed to appeal especially to the 'Christian market'. The following products are genuinely available:

Bible themed organic nutrition bars – all-natural whole-food bars that contain the seven foods of Deuteronomy 8:8. There are five 'themes': Seeds of Samson, Sweet Shalom, Abraham's Bosom, Bar of Judah and Jacob's Ladder. They are produced by Logia in the USA.

T-shirts to tie in with *The Lord of the Rings* movies. The legend says: One King to Rule Them All, One Son to Find Them, One Love to Bring Them All, One Spirit to Bind Them.

Christian T-shirts and sweatshirts produced by The Yahwear Clothing Company (established 1989).

Sacred Nectar – a concoction of royal jelly, pollen and honey whose logo reads 'Mine eyes have been enlightened because I tasted a little bit of this honey' (1 Samuel 14:29).

Thoroughly Cleansed – biblically based detoxifier.

Twelve apostles beer mug – from Tyro International.

Wash Away Your Sins Bubble Bath – from Blue Q.

Jacob's stones from the Jordan River – from the Holy Land Shop.

The Jesus Ashtray – from the Exit 9 Gift Emporium.

Gospel frisbee – available from Slip Disc Ministries.

Almighty Mints – from Hospitality Mints.

CALVINISM

The core of original Calvinism is seen in the following five doctrinal points, known as TULIP:

1 **T**otal depravity   4 **I**rresistible grace

2 **U**nconditional election   5 **P**erseverance of the saints

3 **L**imited atonement

KNOW YOUR NARNIA

THE MAGICIAN'S NEPHEW
Digory and Polly discover a secret passage that links their houses.
They vanish to the world of Charn and meet the lion-king Aslan who
creates Narnia. But the evil enchantress Queen Jadis, who once ruled
Charn, is not far away in this new paradise.

THE LION, THE WITCH AND THE WARDROBE
Peter, Susan, Edmund and Lucy Pevensie find their way into Narnia
through a wardrobe, to find the enchanted land in permanent winter.
The evil White Witch rules over Narnia and the children have to turn
to Aslan to defeat her.

THE HORSE AND HIS BOY
Calormen is a land far to the south of Narnia, where animals cannot talk
and humans can still be treated as slaves. The story takes place before the
adventures in *The Lion, the Witch and the Wardrobe* have ended. A poor fisher-
boy called Shasta dreams of travelling to the north. Then one day, a
Calormene nobleman arrives and demands to buy Shasta from his father.
Amazingly, the Calormene's horse speaks to him. Their journey together
is full of danger and amazing twists and turns of fortune. They meet
Aravis, a young Calormene girl who is also running away, but can they
trust her?

PRINCE CASPIAN
A year after their adventures in *The Lion, the Witch and the Wardrobe*, the
Pevensie children are called back to Narnia to overthrow the evil tyrant
Miraz. The children have to help his nephew, Prince Caspian, in his
quest to restore order in Narnia.

THE VOYAGE OF THE DAWN TREADER
Eustace Scrubb and his cousins Edmund and Lucy are transported to
The Dawn Treader where they meet up with Prince Caspian. Because of
his greed, Eustace is changed into a dragon! Edmund and Lucy are
trapped on Deathwater Island. Aslan is their last hope.

THE SILVER CHAIR

Eustace Scrubb and school friend, Jill Pole, find themselves in Narnia, on a quest to find Prince Caspian's son, Prince Rilian. They are helped by Puddleglum the Marshwiggle, and they meet the Lady of the Green Kirtle, who sends them to the Giants of Harfang.

THE LAST BATTLE

A false Aslan is roaming Narnia, commanding everyone to work for the cruel Calormenes. The last battle is the greatest of all and the final struggle between good and evil. It is up to Eustace and Jill to find the real Aslan and bring his peace for ever to Narnia.

PATRON SAINTS AND FOOTBALL CLUBS

Club	Name	Patron Saint of
Boston United	Nicholas of Myra	Pilgrims
Chester City	John Francis Regis	Illegitimate children
Doncaster Rovers	Agatha	Protection from fire
Dover Athletic	Denys	France
Hartlepool Utd	Cuthbert	Northumbria
Hayes	Gregory	Hopeless cases
Kettering Town	Vitus	Actors
Morecambe	Dympna	The insane
Rushden and Diamonds	Crispin	Shoemakers
Scarborough	Jude	Hopeless cases
Southport	Eloi	Goldsmiths, blacksmiths and farriers
St Mirren	Mirin	Paisley
Stevenage Borough	Felicity	Barren women
Telford United	Joseph	Fathers of families and manual workers
Vale of Leithen	Ronan	Protection from the devil
(Referees	Lucy	The blind)

CHRISTMAS CAROL ORIGINS

Def: **carol**: \Ca'rol\ n.; French *(caroller)*, Latin *(choraula)*, Greek *(choraules)* – to dance around in a circle.

One of the earliest-known Christmas songs is 'Jesus refulsit omnium', composed by St Hilary of Poitiers in the fourth century. During the twelfth century, St Francis of Assisi formally introduced Christmas carols to church services. As patron of the arts, he inspired the composers and poets of the day to deliver Christmas music.

O COME ALL YE FAITHFUL (*ADESTE FIDELES*)
This was a Latin hymn of praise, composed by John Reading in the 1700s. The tune first appeared in the collection known as 'Cantus Diversi' in 1751. The carol was translated into English by Frederick Oakeley.

AWAY IN A MANGER
Also known as Luther's Cradle Hymn, the first two verses were published in 1885. The tune is thought to be from a German folk song.

SILENT NIGHT
This was written in 1818 by Joseph Mohr, an Austrian assistant priest. Informed that the church organ in Nicholas Church in Oberndorf, Austria, was broken, he wrote three stanzas that could be sung by a choir to guitar music. Today, it is the most recorded song of all time.

JINGLE BELLS
This was written by James Pierpont in 1857 for a Thanksgiving service in Boston.

IT CAME UPON A MIDNIGHT CLEAR
Edmund H. Sears, a pastor in Wayland, Massachusetts, wrote this in 1849. The music was provided by Richard S. Willis, then editor of *Musical World*. Uzziah Burnap arranged an accompaniment to the lyrics in 1859.

THE TWELVE DAYS OF CHRISTMAS
This was written in England in the sixteenth century as one of the

'catechism songs' to help young Catholics learn the tenets of their faith.

The 'true love' mentioned in the song refers to God. The 'me' who receives the presents refers to every baptized person. The partridge in a pear tree is Jesus Christ, the Son of God. The other symbols mean the following:

Two turtle doves – the Old and New Testaments

Three French hens – faith, hope and charity, the theological virtues

Four calling birds – the four Gospels and/or the four evangelists

Five gold rings – the first five books of the Old Testament, the Pentateuch

Six geese-a-laying – the six days of creation

Seven swans-a-swimming – the seven gifts of the Holy Spirit, the seven sacraments

Eight maids-a-milking – the eight Beatitudes

Nine ladies dancing – the nine fruits of the Holy Spirit

Ten lords-a-leaping – the ten commandments

Eleven pipers piping – the eleven faithful apostles

Twelve drummers drumming – the twelve points of doctrine in the Apostles' Creed

PSALM 118:8

The shortest chapter in the Bible is Psalm 117.

The longest chapter in the Bible is Psalm 119.

The chapter in the centre of the Bible is Psalm 118.

There are 594 chapters before Psalm 118.

There are 594 chapters after Psalm 118.

Add 594 and 594 and the answer is 1188.

The central verse of the Bible is Psalm 118:8.
'It is better to trust in the Lord than to trust in man.'

UNUSUAL PATRON SAINTS

Name	Patron saint of
Clare of Assisi	Television – an image of the mass appeared on her cell wall when she was too ill to attend the service.
Isidore of Seville	The Internet – he had a prolific writing career which included producing dictionaries, encyclopedias and a history of the world.
Caedwalla of Wales	Serial killers – he killed the pagan inhabitants of the Isle of Wight.
Nicholas of Myra (Turkey)	Pawnbrokers – he paid three bags of gold to save local girls from prostitution.
Monica	Alcoholics – she was a reformed alcoholic.
Blandina	Those falsely accused of cannibalism – she was falsely accused of cannibalism, during the persecutions of Emperor Marcus Aurelius.
Dympna	The mentally ill, runaways and rape victims – her relics are reported to cure the mentally ill and runaways and comfort rape victims.
Drogo	The really ugly – he was stricken with an ugly bodily affliction.
Rose of Viterbo	Those rejected by the monks and nuns – many times, Rose was refused entry to the Poor Clares.
Theobald	Bachelors – he was a hermit, priest and member of the Camaldolese Monks.
Fiacre	Venereal disease – he had a gift of healing.
Philomena	Impossible causes – she healed cancers and heart conditions.
Friad	Spheksophobics (those afraid of wasps) – he prayed for his persecutors to be free from wasp attacks.
Gertrude of Nivelles	Recently deceased – some believed the first day of death was spent in the care of Gertrude.
Drausinus	Invincible people – according to legend, spending a night at the tomb of Drausinus made one invincible.

TWELVE NOAH'S ARK TRUTHS

1. Don't miss the boat.
2. Try to remember that we're all in the same boat.
3. Plan ahead. It wasn't raining when Noah built the ark.
4. Stay fit. When you're 600 years old, someone might ask you to do something *really* big.
5. Don't listen to critics, just get on with what has to be done.
6. Build your future on high ground.
7. For safety's sake, travel in pairs.
8. Two heads are better than one.
9. Speed isn't always an advantage; after all, the snails were on board with the cheetahs.
10. When you're stressed, try floating awhile.
11. Remember that the ark was built by amateurs; it was the Titanic that was built by professionals!
12. No matter what the difficulty, trust in the Almighty: there'll be a rainbow at the end of the storm.

Anon

SEVEN THINGS THAT GOD HATES

There are six things the Lord hates, seven that are detestable to him:

❏ haughty eyes,

❏ a lying tongue,

❏ hands that shed innocent blood,

❏ a heart that devises wicked schemes,

❏ feet that are quick to rush into evil,

❏ a false witness who pours out lies,

❏ and a man who stirs up dissension among brothers.

Proverbs 6:16-19

WHEN I SAY

When I say, 'I am a Christian,'
I'm not shouting, 'I've been saved!'
I'm whispering, 'I get lost!
That's why I chose this way.'

When I say, 'I am a Christian,'
I don't speak with human pride.
I'm confessing that I stumble –
needing God to be my guide.

When I say, 'I am a Christian,'
I'm not trying to be strong.
I'm professing that I'm weak
and pray for strength to carry on.

When I say, 'I am a Christian,'
I'm not bragging of success.
I'm admitting that I've failed
and cannot ever pay the debt.

When I say, 'I am a Christian,'
I don't think I know it all.
I submit to my confusion,
asking humbly to be taught.

When I say, 'I am a Christian,'
I'm not claiming to be perfect.
My flaws are too visible,
but God believes I'm worth it.

When I say, 'I am a Christian,'
I still feel the sting of pain.
I have my share of heartache,
which is why I seek his name.

When I say, 'I am a Christian,'
I do not wish to judge.
I have no authority…
I only know I'm loved.

Carol Wimmer

CHRISTIAN VEGETARIAN ASSOCIATION MISSION

1. To **support** and encourage Christian vegetarians around the world.

2. To **share** with non-vegetarian Christians how a vegetarian diet can add meaning to one's faith, aid in one's spirituality and enhance one's moral life.

3. To **show** the world that plant-based diets represent good, responsible Christian stewardship for all God's creation.

THE ALPHA COURSE

The Alpha Course is a 15-session practical introduction to the Christian faith, aimed at people who don't go to church. The syllabus for the course is in the book *Questions of Life* by Nicky Gumbel, from Holy Trinity Church, Brompton, England. Each session consists of a meal, a talk and a discussion around a key topic. The topics are:

1. Christianity: boring, untrue and irrelevant?
2. Who is Jesus?
3. Why did Jesus die?
4. How can I be sure of my faith?
5. Why and how should I read the Bible?
6. Why and how do I pray?
7. How does God guide us?
8. Who is the Holy Spirit?
9. What does the Holy Spirit do?
10. How can I be filled with the Spirit?
11. How can I resist evil?
12. Why and how should we tell others?
13. Does God heal today?
14. What about the church?
15. How can I make the most of the rest of my life?

The growth of the Alpha Course has been prolific. In 1991, just four churches were running the course. Today, well over six million people across the world have taken the Alpha Course in 28,000 churches of all denominations. The Alpha Course promotes itself in many ways – in the UK, primarily through an annual advertising initiative, involving billboards, bus posters, church noticeboards and radio commercials. The Alpha Course is introducing people to the Christian faith in 144 countries, including the USA, Australia, Canada, Germany, Switzerland and Japan.

THE PLIAN GOESPL

Aocdrnicg to rsecareh at Cmbagrdie Uinervtisy, it denos't mtater waht oredr the ltteers in a wrod are in, the olny iprmoatnt tihng is taht the frist and lsat ltteer be at the rghit pclae. The rset can be a taotl mses and you can sitll raed it wouthit porbelm. Tihs is bcuseae the huamn mnid deos not raed ervey lteter by istlef, but the wrod as a wlohe.

For God so leovd the wrlod taht he gvae his olny bttegoen son, that woehvesor belvetieh in him sholud not peisrh, but htah evlerainstg lfie. *Anon*

NAMES OF JESUS

And he shall be called...
Advocate (1 John 2:1);
   The Lamb of God (John 1:29);
      The resurrection and the life; (John 11:25);
         Judge of the living and the dead (Acts 10:42);
            Lord of lords (1 Timothy 6:15);
               Man of sorrows (Isaiah 53:3);
                  Head of the church (Ephesians 5:23);
                     Master (Matthew 8:19).
The faithful and true witness (Revelation 3:14);
   Rock (1 Corinthians 10:4);
      A high priest (Hebrews 6:20);
         The gate (John 10:9);
            Living water (John 4:10);
               The bread of life (John 6:35);
                  A rose of Sharon (Song of Solomon 2:1);
                     The Alpha and the Omega (Revelation 22:13).
The true vine (John 15:1);
   The Anointed One (Daniel 9:25);
      A Teacher (John 3:2);
         The Holy One of God(Mark 1:24);
            Mediator (1 Timothy 2:5);
               The One he loves (Ephesians 1:6);
                  A branch (Isaiah 11:1);
                     Light of the world (John 8:12).
The image of the invisible God (Colossians 1:15);
   The Word (John 1:1);
      Chief Cornerstone (Ephesians 2:20);
         Saviour (John 4:42);
            Servant (Matthew 12:18);
               Author & Finisher of Our Faith (Hebrews 12:2);
                  The Almighty (Revelation 1:8)
Lion of the Tribe of Judah (Revelation 5:5);
   Prince of Peace (Isaiah 9:6);
      Bridegroom (Matthew 9:15);
         Only Begotten Son (John 3:16);
            Immanuel (Isaiah 7:14);
               The Amen (Revelation 3:14)

BIBLICAL SONGS

Noah: 'Raindrops Keep Falling on My Head'

Joseph: 'Any Dream Will Do'

Goliath: 'Another One Bites the Dust'

Adam and Eve: 'I Feel Free'

Stephen: 'Tears in Heaven'

Esther: 'Wonderful Tonight'

Job: 'I've Got a Right to Sing the Blues'

Lazarus: 'Please Release Me'

Samson: 'Delilah'

Salome: 'I Could Have Danced All Night'

Daniel: 'The Lion Sleeps Tonight'

Joshua: 'Good Vibrations'

Peter: 'Keys to Your Love'

Esau: 'Born to Be Wild'

Shadrach, Meshach and Abednego: 'Great Balls of Fire!'

Jonah: 'Gimme Shelter'

Elijah: 'Up, Up and Away'

Methuselah: 'Stayin' Alive'

Nebuchadnezzar: 'Crazy'

Judas: 'My Way'

Enoch: 'The Happy Wanderer'

James: 'We Can Work it Out'

Jude: 'Hey Jude'

Nehemiah: 'Another Brick in the Wall'

Satan: 'Sympathy for the Devil'

Jezebel: 'Under My Thumb'

Paul: 'Losing My Religion'

Jeremiah: 'Worried Life Blues'

CHRISTIANITY IN SIXTEENTH-CENTURY JAPAN

1549: Jesuit missionary Francis Xavier establishes Japan's first Christian mission at Kagoshima.

1563: Jesuit missionary Luis Frois arrives in Japan; he later writes *Historia de Japan*, which covers the years 1549–93. Omura Sumitada becomes the first convert.

1571: The first Portuguese merchant ship arrives to trade at Nagasaki.

1578: Otomo Sorin, a Japanese lord, is baptized under the name Francisco.

1579: Alessandro Valignano, supervisor of the Jesuit missions in Asia, arrives in Japan.

1580: Daimyo (Great Lord) Arima Harunobu becomes a Christian and takes the name Protasio.

1582: Four Christian Japanese boys are sent to Rome at the urging of Alessandro Valignano for an audience with Pope Gregory XIII (Mission To Europe of 1582).

1587: Toyotomi Hideyoshi, a leading samurai, issues an edict expelling all Christian missionaries; it is not obeyed or enforced.

1596: The San Felipe Incident: Toyotomi Hideyoshi confiscates the Spanish galleon San Felipe, inaugurating his persecution of Catholic missionaries.

1597: Twenty-six Japanese and foreign Christians are crucified at Nagasaki by order of Toyotomi Hideyoshi.

1598: Toyotomi Hideyoshi dies.

CREED \KREED\

Def: **Creed:**\kreed\n.; ME (*crede*), from OE (*creeda*), Latin (*credo*), 'I believe', the first word of the Apostles' and Nicene Creeds, from *credere* – to believe, trust, entrust; akin to OIr *cretid* 'he believes'.

1. a brief authoritative formula of religious belief.
2. a set of fundamental beliefs.
3. a guiding principle.

The 'Rule of Faith' as recorded by Irenaeus (early Church Father):

> this faith: in one God, the Father Almighty, who made the
> heaven and the earth and the seas and all the things that are in
> them; and in one Christ Jesus, the Son of God, who was made
> flesh for our salvation; and in the Holy Spirit, who made known
> through the prophets the plan of salvation, and the coming, and
> the birth from a virgin, and the passion, and the resurrection
> from the dead, and the bodily ascension into heaven of the
> beloved Christ Jesus, our Lord, and his future appearing from
> heaven in the glory of the Father to sum up all things and to
> raise anew all flesh of the whole human race...

An account of the baptismal service by Hippolytus (early Church Father):

> When the person being baptized goes down into the water, he
> who baptizes him, putting his hand on him, shall say: 'Do you
> believe in God, the Father Almighty?' And the person being
> baptized shall say: 'I believe.' Then holding his hand on his head,
> he shall baptize him once. And then he shall say: 'Do you believe
> in Christ Jesus, the Son of God, who was born of the Virgin
> Mary, and was crucified under Pontius Pilate, and was dead and
> buried, and rose again the third day, alive from the dead, and
> ascended into heaven, and sat at the right hand of the Father,
> and will come to judge the living and the dead?' And when he
> says: 'I believe,' he is baptized again. And again he shall say: 'Do
> you believe in the Holy Spirit, in the holy church, and the
> resurrection of the body?' The person being baptized shall say:
> 'I believe,' and then he is baptized a third time.

DEALING WITH DISAPPOINTMENT

Disappointment – his appointment,
change one letter, then I see
that the thwarting of my purpose
is God's better choice for me.
His appointment must be blessing,
though it may come in disguise,
for the end from the beginning
open to his wisdom lies.
Anon

THE BIBLE IN FIFTY WORDS

There are 775,632 words in the Authorized Version or King James Bible. This is the condensed version:

God made, Adam bit, Noah arked, Abraham split, Joseph ruled, Jacob fooled, bush talked, Moses balked; Pharaoh plagued, people walked. Sea divided, tablets guided, promise landed. Saul freaked, David peeked, prophets warned, Jesus born. God walked, love talked, anger crucified, hope died. Love rose, Spirit flamed, word spread, God remained.
Anon

SUNDAY OBSERVANCE

The earliest evidence for spending the first day of the week in remembrance of Christ's resurrection is found in the Pauline period. Old Testament custom kept the Sabbath, but with some freedom (and paradoxically, extreme limitation) as to the method of its observance. At first, daily meetings were held for the expression of thanks for salvation. But soon a movement began among Gentile Christians (compare 1 Corinthians 16:2 with Acts 20:7) to hold longer services on Sunday, characterized in part by the collection of free-will offerings. The name, 'the Lord's Day', became a designation for it (Revelation 1:10). The day is called Sunday by Justin Martyr *as commemorating* the creation of light on the first day of the creation and also the awakening of Christ, the 'Sun of righteousness', from the darkness of the grave.

DETERMINING THE DATE OF EASTER

Easter Sunday is the Sunday following the first full moon of spring, known as the Paschal Full Moon (PFM). In June AD 325, astronomers approximated astronomical full-moon dates for the Christian church, calling them Ecclesiastical Full Moon (EFM) dates. From AD 326, the PFM date has always been the EFM date after 20 March (which was the equinox date in AD 325).

According to this calculation, the earliest possible date for Easter is 22 March and the latest is April. The following table gives the date for Easter for the next 10 years:

Year	Easter Day
2005	27 March
2006	16 April
2007	8 April
2008	23 March
2009	12 April
2010	4 April
2011	24 April
2012	8 April
2013	31 March
2014	20 April

ST PATRICK'S LORICA
(MORNING PRAYER OF ST PATRICK)(edited version)

I arise today
through a mighty strength, the invocation of the Trinity,
through a belief in the Threeness,
through confession of the Oneness
of the Creator of creation.

I arise today
through the strength of Christ's birth and his baptism,
through the strength of his crucifixion and his burial,
through the strength of his resurrection and his ascension,
through the strength of his descent for the judgment of doom…

I arise today
through the strength of heaven;
light of the sun,
splendour of fire,
speed of lightning,
swiftness of the wind,
depth of the sea,
stability of the earth,
firmness of the rock.

I arise today
through God's strength to pilot me,
God's might to uphold me,
God's wisdom to guide me,
God's eye to look before me,
God's ear to hear me,
God's word to speak for me,
God's hand to guard me,
God's way to lie before me,
God's shield to protect me,
God's hosts to save me
from snares of the devil,
from temptations of vices,
from every one who desires me ill,
afar and anear,
alone or in a multitude.

Christ with me, Christ before me, Christ behind me,
Christ in me, Christ beneath me, Christ above me,
Christ on my right, Christ on my left,
Christ when I lie down, Christ when I sit down,
Christ in the heart of every man who thinks of me,
Christ in the mouth of every man who speaks of me,
Christ in the eye that sees me,
Christ in the ear that hears me.
 St Patrick (c. 377)

THE CHRISTIAN ORIGINS OF BASKETBALL

James Naismith, a Presbyterian minister, invented basketball in 1891,
while employed as a YMCA physical director at their International
Training School in Springfield, Massachusetts. He used a football and
fixed half-bushel peach baskets to both ends of the Springfield gym. His
18-member class was split into two opposing teams and coached to toss
the ball into their opponent's basket. After some experimentation,
Naismith refined the game to its current form: two five-player teams,
a ball four inches larger in circumference than a football and hoops with
nets and backboards.

Naismith published basketball rules in 1892 and, by 1896, the game had reached England, France, Brazil, Australia, China and India. By 1897, the game was so popular in North America that the YMCA started banning it because teams were monopolizing their gyms. At the 1936 Berlin Games, basketball became the first team sport in Olympic competition.

A spiritual giant, Naismith had this advice for teams playing his game: 'Let us be able to lose gracefully and to win courteously; to accept criticism as well as praise; and to appreciate the attitude of the other fellow at all times.'

At his Springfield interview, he was asked, 'What is the work of a YMCA physical director?' He answered, 'To win men for the Master through the gym.'

CHRISTIAN SURFERS OF AUSTRALIA

Christian Surfers of Australia exist to be a Christian presence and witness to the entire Australian surfing community.

VISION

To link the entire Australian coastline with local Christian Surfers ministries.

CORE VALUES

Evangelism: Evangelistic in intent, majoring on Christ, the gospel and the Bible.

Surfers: Mobilizing surfers to reach other surfers, with a culturally relevant message.

Surfing: Submission to Christ through servanthood, rather than serving the sport of surfing through selfish ambition.

Community: Creating a Christian community for outreach.

Church: Locally based and accountable through many Christian church denominations.

Kingdom mindedness: Transforming the wider surfing culture by individual conversions as well as influencing the surfing subculture.

Partnerships: Working with God and what he is already doing through others, while respecting and partnering with other ministries.

Servanthood: Serving others through relationships.

Grassroots: Empowering and developing the local ministry level.

Volunteer based: Helping Christian volunteers fulfill their God-given calling and potential.

STRANGE BIBLE VERSIONS

1562 PLACEMAKER'S BIBLE
Substitutes 'placemakers' for 'peacemakers' in the Sermon on the Mount, to read, 'Blessed are the placemakers, for they shall be called the children of God' (Matthew 5:9).

1611 JUDAS BIBLE
Has Judas instead of Jesus in the Garden of Gethsemane saying to his disciples, 'Sit here ye, while I go and pray yonder' (Matthew 26:36).

1631 THE WICKED BIBLE
Also known as the 'Adulterer's Bible' because it leaves the 'not' out of the seventh commandment so that it reads 'Thou shalt commit adultery.' King Charles fined the printers £300 and ordered all copies to be destroyed.

1641 MORE SEA BIBLE
Rendered Revelation 21:1 (And there was no more sea) as 'there was more sea'!

1638 THE FOOLISH BIBLE
A typographical mistake led to Psalm 14:1 reading, 'The fool has said in his heart there is a God,' instead of 'The fool says in his heart, "There is no God."' Printers were fined £3,000 this time, and all copies were destroyed.

1653 THE UNRIGHTEOUS BIBLE
This version contains two unfortunate mistakes. It omits the second 'not' from the question in 1 Corinthians 6:9, which should read: 'Do you not know that the wicked will *not* inherit the kingdom of God?' And it renders Romans 6:13 as: 'Neither yield ye your members as instruments of righteousness unto sin.' Of course, it should read *'unrighteousness'*.

1801 MURDERER'S BIBLE

Mistakenly puts in 'murderers' instead of 'murmurers' in Jude 1:16, so it reads, 'these men are *murderers* and faultfinders…'.

I ASKED GOD FOR STRENGTH

I asked God for strength,
that I might achieve;
I was made weak,
that I might learn humbly to obey.
I asked for health,
that I might do great things.
I was given infirmity,
that I might do better things.
I asked for riches,
that I might be happy;
I was given poverty,
that I might be wise.
I asked for power,
that I might have the praise of men;
I was given weakness,
that I might feel the need for God.
I asked for all things,
that I might enjoy life;
I was given life,
that I might enjoy all things.
I got nothing that I asked for;
but everything I had hoped for.
Almost despite myself
my unspoken prayers were answered.
I am among all men,
most richly blessed.
Anon

OCCUPATIONS AND PATRON SAINTS

This is a notoriously difficult area because many occupations have more than one saint, as occupations subdivide into specialities and more saints may be attached to jobs over time.

Occupation	Saint
Gardeners	Adam
Scientists	Albert the Great
Brewers, hotelkeepers	Amand
Fishermen	Andrew and Peter
Miners	Anne
Dentists	Apollonia
Theologians	Augustine
Bankers	Bernadino (Feltre)
Advertisers	Bernadino of Siena
Nurses	Camillus de Lellis
Cobblers, shoemakers (and leather-workers)	Crispinian
Poets	David
Astronomers	Dominic
Florists	Dorothy
Merchants	Francis of Assisi
Sailors	Francis of Paola
Soldiers	George and Joan of Arc
Tailors	Homobonus
Bakers	Honoratus
Farmers	Isidore the Farmer
Carpenters	Joseph
Gravediggers, undertakers	Joseph of Arimathea
Astronauts	Joseph of Copertino

NOBEL CHRISTIANS

The whole of my remaining realizable estate shall be dealt with in the following way: the capital, invested in safe securities by my executors, shall constitute a fund, the interest on which shall be annually distributed in the form of prizes to those who, during the preceding year, shall have conferred the greatest benefit on mankind.
From the will of Alfred Nobel, founder of the Nobel Prize

The Nobel Prize consists of a medal, 10 million Swedish krone (2003) and a personal diploma. Prizes are awarded each year in six categories: peace, literature, physics, chemistry, medicine and economics (since 1968). Christians and Christian organizations that have been recognized by the Nobel Prize Committee include:

Nobel Laureate	Category	Year	Nationality
Ernesto Teodoro Moneta (shared with Louis Renault)	Peace	1907	Italian
Klas Pontus Arnoldson (shared with Fredrik Bajer)	Peace	1908	Swedish
Wladyslaw Reymont	Literature	1924	Polish
Archbishop Lars Olof Jonathan (Nathan) Söderblom	Peace	1930	Swedish
Arthur Henderson	Peace	1934	British
John R. Mott (shared with Emily Greene Balch)	Peace	1946	American
The Quakers	Peace	1947	British and American
Thomas Stearns Eliot	Literature	1948	British
Albert Schweitzer	Peace	1952	French
Winston Churchill	Literature	1953	British
Georges Pire	Peace	1958	Belgian
Martin Luther King Jr	Peace	1964	American
Mother Teresa	Peace	1979	Macedonian
Archbishop Desmond Mpilo Tutu	Peace	1984	South African
Carlos Filipe Ximenes Belo (shared with José Ramos-Horta)	Peace	1996	East Timorese
Jimmy Carter	Peace	2002	American

IMMOVABLE GREAT FEASTS OF THE
RUSSIAN ORTHODOX CHURCH

Feast	Julian Year	Gregorian Year
Nativity of the Theotokos (Mother of God) – birth of Mary	8 September	21 September
Elevation of the Cross – strict fasting in remembrance of the suffering of Christ	14 September	27 September
Presentation of the Theotokos in the Temple – to remember that children are a gift from God	21 November	4 December
Nativity of Christ – the coming of Emmanuel	25 December	7 January
Theophany – baptism of the Lord	6 January	19 January
Presentation of Christ in the Temple – recalls the faithful witnesses, Simeon and Anna	2 February	15 February
Annunciation – the proclamation of Gabriel	25 March	7 April
Transfiguration of the Lord – the proof of the Lord's divinity	6 August	19 August
Dormition (death) of the Theotokos – celebration of the death and resurrection of Mary	15 August	28 August

LONGEST AND SHORTEST PAPAL REIGNS

Longest	Shortest
Pius IX (1846–78): 31 years and 7 months	Urban VII (15 September – 27 September 1590): 13 calendar days
John Paul II (1978–present): 25 years and 10 months as of 16 August 2004	Boniface VI (April, 896): 16 calendar days
Leo XIII (1878–1903): 25 years and 5 months	Celestine IV (25 October – 10 November 1241): 17 calendar days
Pope Pius VI (1775–99): 24 years and 6 months	Sisinnius (15 January – 4 February 708): 21 calendar days
Adrian I (772–95): 23 years and 10 months	Theodore II (December 897): 21 calendar days
Pius VII (1800–23): 23 years and 5 months.	Marcellus II (10 April – 1 May 1555): 22 calendar days
Alexander III (1159–81): 21 years, 11 months, and 23 days.	Damasus II (17 July – 9 August 1048): 24 calendar days
St Silvester I (314–35): 21 years and 11 months	Pius III (22 September – 18 October 1503): 27 calendar days
St Leo I (440–61): 21 years and 1 month	Leo XI (1 April – 27 April 1605: 27 calendar days
Urban VIII (1623–44): almost 21 years	Pope Benedict V (22 May – 23 June 964): 33 calendar days

LOST BOOKS

There are several books referred to in the Bible that are not in the Bible:

Subject	Bible Reference
Book of the Wars of the Lord	Numbers 21:14
Book of Jashar	Joshua 10:13
The Acts of Solomon	1 Kings 11:41
Annals of the Kings of Israel	1 Kings 14:19
Annals of the Kings of Judah	1 Kings 14:29
The Kings of Israel	1 Chronicles 9:1
Records of the Seer Samuel	1 Chronicles 29:29
Records of the Prophet Nathan	1 Chronicles 29:29
Records of the Seer Gad	1 Chronicles 29:29
Prophecy of Ahijah the Shilonite	2 Chronicles 9:29
Visions of the Seer Iddo	2 Chronicles 9:29
Records of the Prophet Shemaiah and the Seer Iddo	2 Chronicles 12:15
Story of the Prophet Iddo	2 Chronicles 13:22
Book of the Kings of Judah and Israel	2 Chronicles 16:11
Annals of Jehu son of Hanani	2 Chronicles 20:34
Commentary on the Book of the Kings	2 Chronicles 24:27
Acts of Uzziah	2 Chronicles 26:22
Book of the Kings of Israel and Judah	2 Chronicles 27:7
Record of the Seers	2 Chronicles 33:19
Book of the Annals	Nehemiah 12:23

JESUS ON FILM

Many facets of Jesus' life have been given the film treatment. Some are bizarre and others accord well with the record of scripture. Like any art form, film is limited by many factors such as time, culture, money and audience. It is fair to say that no one film entirely captures Jesus' humanity, divinity and eternal relevance. However, that has not stopped film producers from having a go! Films about Jesus include:

Film	Strengths	Limitations
Intolerance (1916)	A human portrayal	Too many subplots
The King of Kings (1927)	Miracles	No words
Ben Hur (1959)	Supernatural dimension emphasized	Jesus not on screen!
King of Kings (1961)	Great soundtrack	Slow moving
The Greatest Story Ever Told (1965)	Humanity highlighted	Miracles understated
Jesus Christ Superstar (1972)	Shows Jesus for the rock generation	No resurrection
Godspell (1973)	Catchy tunes	No resurrection
Jesus of Nazareth (1977)	Powerful crucifixion scenes	Shown over a number of weeks, not as one film
The Life of Brian (1979)	Comedy treatment of religious intolerance	Bad-taste mistaken-identity comedy
The Jesus Film (1979)	Straightforward adaptation of Gospel accounts	Lack of secular take up
The Last Temptation of Christ (1988)	Some moving miracles	Christ becomes a sinner
Jesus of Montreal (1989)	Modern adaptation	Downplays miracles
Jesus: The Mini Series (2000)	Warm presentation	Mini-series format
The Passion of the Christ (2004)	A faithful rendition of the last 12 hours of Jesus' life	Jewish lobby not happy

THE TWELVE RULES OF GOOD PURITAN BEHAVIOUR

1. Profane no divine ordinance.
2. Touch no state matters.
3. Urge no healths.
4. Pick no quarrels.
5. Encourage no vice.
6. Repeat no grievances.
7. Reveal no secrets.
8. Maintain no ill opinions.
9. Make no comparisons.
10. Keep no bad company.
11. Make no long meals.
12. Lay no wagers.

INEXACT OLD TESTAMENT REFERENCES

References to the Old Testament in the New Testament are mostly precise. However, in some cases it is not possible to find an exact reference (often because of inexact translation). For example, Matthew 2:23 has the statement (referring to Jesus) – 'So was fulfilled what was said through the prophets: "He will be called a Nazarene".' (New International Version). This exact term is not found in any prophecy. However, Jerome links 'Nazarene' with the Hebrew word *Nezer* ('sprout') and identifies it with 'the Branch', the term designated to the Messiah by Isaiah – 'A shoot will come up from the stump of Jesse; from his roots a Branch will bear fruit' (Isaiah 11:1).

Some other 'terminological inexactitudes' are given on the right.

NEW TESTAMENT	OLD TESTAMENT VERSION
MATTHEW 5:5	**PSALM 37:11**
Blessed are the meek, for they will inherit the earth.	But the meek will inherit the land and enjoy great peace.
MARK 13:31	**ISAIAH 40:8**
Heaven and earth will pass away, but my words will never pass away.	The grass withers and the flowers fall, but the word of our God stands forever.
LUKE 1:79	**ISAIAH 9:2**
…to shine on those living in darkness and in the shadow of death, to guide our feet into the path of peace.	The people walking in darkness have seen a great light; on those living in the land of the shadow of death a light has dawned.
JOHN 4:37	**MICAH 6:15**
Thus the saying 'One sows and another reaps' is true.	You will plant but not harvest; you will press olives but not use the oil on yourselves; you will crush grapes but not drink the wine.
ACTS 10:34	**JOB 34:19**
Then Peter began to speak: 'I now realise how true it is that God does not show favouritism…'	…who shows no partiality to princes and does not favour the rich over the poor…
ROMANS 11:8	**ISAIAH 29:11**
…as it is written: 'God gave them a spirit of stupor, eyes so that they could not see and ears so that they could not hear, to this very day.'	For you this whole vision is nothing but words sealed in a scroll. And if you give the scroll to someone who can read, and say to him, 'Read this, please,' he will answer, 'I can't; it is sealed.'

ALTERNATIVE BIBLICAL NAMES

The Puritans relied heavily on Old Testament names for their progeny to distinguish them from the godless masses. As a result, many strange names began to appear in America, where the Puritans settled after the arrival of *The Mayflower* in 1620. Classic examples include: Given, Praise-God, Desire, Love, Much-Merceye, Increased, Sin-denie, Fearnot, Renewed, Safe-on-high and Repentance. There was hardly a name in the Bible that was not used, regardless of its associations, even though the more conservative religious leaders did not encourage their use. Instead, they recommended using the names of virtuous people found in the scriptures. Popular naming patterns for several siblings included Hope, Faith, Charity and Patience.

Three biblical female names are commonly found in early New England: Jemimah, Keziah and Keren-happuch – the daughters of Job. If people researched their family trees, they might discover ancestors named Antipas, Cain, Bezaleel, Habakkuk or Bathsheba!

MARTIN LUTHER: KEY DATES

1483: Luther was born on 10 November at Eisleben and was baptized the following day.

1501: Luther entered the university in Erfurt and received his bachelor's degree one year later. Three years later, he graduated as Master of Arts.

1505: He vowed to St Anne that he would become a monk and give his life to the Roman Catholic Church after a brush with death in a thunderstorm. He gave away his earthly possessions and entered the Augustinian monastery in Erfurt. He thought that by making this sacrifice he would earn peace with God.

1507: Ordained a Roman Catholic priest, he was (he believed) endowed by the pope with the awesome power to forgive and retain sins and to administer the sacraments.

1508: He taught philosophy at the University of Wittenberg. He continued to be troubled by his sins and saw no solution to his guilt and no way to satisfy God's requirements but through his own works of merit, sacrifices and penances.

1510: He made a pilgrimage to Rome, travelling on foot some 850 miles, hoping there to have his doubts of salvation removed. He was shocked by the abuses he saw there and returned to Wittenberg more confused than ever.

1512: He earned the degree of Doctor of Theology, the highest degree for a student of the Bible.

1514: Luther found salvation by accepting Romans 1:16–17. He believed that poor sinners could never find peace with God by their own works. God, in Christ, had done everything to save them as his free gift to the undeserving. This gift was received only by faith, only by confidence in God's mercy, without the deeds of the Law; and even saving faith itself was God's gift through the means of the gospel.

1517: On 31 October, Luther nailed his 95 Theses or statements to the church door in Wittenberg, questioning the church's sale of forgiveness in letters of indulgence. This was the start of the Lutheran Reformation.

1520: The pope excommunicated him from the church, branding him a false teacher, a traitor and a heathen. Luther publicly burned the letter in open defiance of the pope and his claim of power over God's Word.

1521: Charles V, the emperor, sought to resolve the rift by hauling Luther before a conference of princes, dukes and bishops of the church in the city of Worms. At this meeting, the pope's representative demanded that Luther take back everything he had written and gave him 24 hours to think it over. The penalty for refusing would mean death for Luther. Luther refused, saying that his conscience was captive to God's word. The next day he was duly banned from preaching. On his way back to Wittenberg, Luther was kidnapped by friends and hidden away safely in a castle called the Wartburg near Eisenach. There he stayed in disguise for almost a year and translated the New Testament into German for his people. His complete German bible was published in 1534.

1546: Luther died on 18 February at Eisleben.

JOHN DONNE

John Donne was born in London in 1572. Famous for his spellbinding sermons, he was the most outstanding of the English Metaphysical Poets. Although from a prominent Roman Catholic family, he converted to Anglicanism in his twenties. He entered the University of Oxford at 11, and then went on to study law at the University of Cambridge. Donne was appointed private secretary to Sir Thomas Egerton, Keeper of the Great Seal, in 1598 and secretly married Egerton's niece, Anne More, in 1601. This resulted in him losing his job and in a brief period of imprisonment. In 1615, John Donne became an Anglican priest and was appointed Royal Chaplain later that year. In 1621, he was named dean of St Paul's Cathedral, London. He attained eminence as a preacher, delivering sermons that are regarded as the most brilliant and eloquent of his time.

RESURRECTION, IMPERFECT

Sleep, sleep, old Sun, thou canst not have repass'd
As yet, the wound thou took'st on Friday last;
Sleep then, and rest; the world may bear thy stay,
A better sun rose before thee to-day,
Who – not content to enlighten all that dwell
On the earth's face, as thou – enlightened hell
And made the dark fires languish in that vale,
As at thy presence here our fires grow pale;
Whose body, having walk'd on earth, and now
Hasting to heaven, would that he might allow
Himself unto all stations, and fill all
For these three days become a mineral;
He was all gold when he lay down, but rose
All tincture, and doth not alone dispose
Leaden and iron wills to good, but is
Of power to make e'en sinful flesh like his.
Had one of those, whose credulous piety
Thought that a soul one might discern and see
Go from a body, at this sepulchre been,
And, issuing from the sheet, this body seen,
He would have justly thought this body a soul,
If not of any man, yet of the whole.

A HARMONIOUS BIBLE

Unlike any other book, the Bible has a unique harmony. Compare, for example, the first and last books, Genesis and Revelation:

Genesis	Revelation
Book of beginning	Book of the end
Earth created (1:1)	Earth passes away (21:1)
Satan's first rebellion (3:1–5)	Satan's final rebellion (20: 7-10)
Sun, moon and stars to govern the earth (1:14–18)	Sun, moon and stars connected with earth's judgment (6:13; 8:12; 16:8)
Sun governs the day (1:16)	No need of the sun (21:23)
Humans created in God's image (1:26)	God lives with people (or humankind), his children (21:3, 7)
Entrance of sin (3:4-7)	End of sin (21:4, 8; 22:14–15)
Curse pronounced (3:14, 17)	No more curse (22:3)
Sorrow and suffering enter (3:17–19)	No more sorrow or crying (21:4)
Marriage of the first Adam, (2:18–24)	Marriage of the last Adam (19:1–9)
Two angels act on behalf of God and his people (19:1–38)	Two witnesses act on behalf of God and his people (11:1–12)
Promised seed to possess cities of his enemies (22:17–18)	Promised seed comes into possession of the earth and his kingdom (11:18)
Man's dominion ceases and Satan's begins (3:23–24)	Satan's dominion ends and the eternal sons of God are restored to the Kingdom (22:1–21)
Old serpent causes sin, suffering and death (3:1–24)	Old serpent bound for 1,000 years (20:1–3)
Doom of the old serpent pronounced (3:14–15)	Doom on the old serpent executed (20:10)
Sun, moon and stars associated with Israel (37:9)	Sun, moon and stars associated with Israel again (12:1–20
Jacob's trouble (32:6–7)	Great tribulation (6:9–11, 7:14)

GIDEONS INTERNATIONAL

Founded in 1899 in America, to 'win men, women, boys and girls to the Lord Jesus Christ', this non-profit organization freely distributes one million copies of the Word of God every seven days (or 112 per minute). Bibles are placed, free of charge, in hotels, nursing homes, prisons, hospitals and military units. Students at school, college and university, as well as police, fire fighters, nursing staff and emergency medical teams, are offered free Bibles by local volunteers.

The Gideons International ministry covers over 170 countries and in the fiscal year ending 31 May 2003 it received nearly 98 million US dollars in total income. Nearly 90 million US dollars were used to purchase 60.3 million scriptures (Bibles and New Testaments) in over 70 languages in the 179 countries where the Gideons are organized. Many thousands of people have been impacted by this ministry in needy areas such as Turkey, Tanzania, Hungary, Romania and Belarus.

THE CHURCH IN KOREA

It is a remarkable fact that one of the most Christianized countries in the world, South Korea, is juxtaposed with one of the most anti-Christian nations, North Korea. In the late seventeenth century, Jesuits from China were influential in proclaiming Christianity to Korean Buddhist monks. The Korean Catholic Church was born in 1777 and started to evangelize right from the start. The 'Sinyu Persecution' of 1801, in which 300 Christians were martyred, was the first major persecution of Catholics in Korea. In another persecution in 1866, 8,000 Christians were slain by the authorities.

Protestant missions to Korea began with increasing openness in the late nineteenth century, and in 1899, the state proclaimed religious freedom. However, from 1901 to 1945, Korea was occupied by Japan and Christianity was banned.

In the 1950s, churches that had been closed were re-established, but in 1953 the nation was divided into North and South Korea. Under American control, the South Korean Church flourished. Kim Il-Sung was installed as a Marxist dictator by the Soviets in North Korea. Churches were destroyed and Christians martyred in their thousands. Ironically, Pyongyang, the North Korean capital, was once such a place of Christian revival that it was nicknamed 'The Jerusalem of the East'.

Carrying a Bible in North Korea today could lead to execution. Christian worship or association of any kind could lead to lengthy imprisonment in concentration camps.

The only religion permitted in North Korea today is the worship of the late 'Eternal President' Kim Il-sung and of his son, the 'Dear Leader' Kim Jong-il.

> Be faithful, even to the point of death,
> and I will give you the crown of life.
> *Revelation 2:10*

PILGRIM'S PROGRESS IN THE SIMILITUDE OF A DREAM – JOHN BUNYAN

CHRISTIAN'S SONG AT THE CROSS
Thus far did I come laden with my sin;
and nothing eased the grief that I was in,
Till I came here; oh, what a place is this!
here must be the starting of my bliss!
Here the burden fell from off my back!
Here the strings that bound it to me cracked!
Blest Cross! Blest Tomb! Blest rather be
the man that there was put to shame for me!

THE WISDOM OF AGUR

There are three things that are never satisfied, four that never say, 'Enough!': **the grave, the barren womb, land**, which is never satisfied with water, and **fire**, which never says, 'Enough!'...

There are three things that are too amazing for me, four that I do not understand: the way of **an eagle** in the sky, the way of **a snake** on a rock, the way of a **ship** on the high seas, and the way of **a man** with a maiden...

Under three things the earth trembles, under four it cannot bear up: **a servant** who becomes king, **a fool** who is full of food, **an unloved woman** who is married, and **a maidservant** who displaces her mistress.

Four things on earth are small, yet they are extremely wise. **Ants** are creatures of little strength, yet they store up their food in the summer; **conies** are creatures of little power, yet they make their home in the crags; **locusts** have no king, yet they advance together in ranks; **a lizard** can be caught with the hand, yet it is found in kings' palaces.

There are three things that are stately in their stride, four that move with stately bearing: **a lion**, mighty among beasts, who retreats before nothing; **a strutting rooster, a he-goat,** and **a king** with his army around him.

Proverbs 30:15–16, 18–19, 21–23

SPIRITUAL GARDENING

Plant:

Four rows of peas:
    Patience
    Perseverance
    Promise
    Prayer

Four rows of squash:
    Squash gossip
    Squash indifference
    Squash self-pity
    Squash bitterness

Four rows of lettuce:
    Let us be unselfish
    Let us love
    Let us give
    Let us rejoice

Four rows of turnips:
    Turn up for church
    Turn up promptly
    Turn up to serve
    Turn up to praise

Anon

IRELAND'S APOSTLE OF TEMPERANCE

Almost single-handedly, a Capuchin friar, Father Theobald Matthew (1790–1856), persuaded over five million Irish men, women and children to abstain totally from alcohol throughout the 1830s and 1840s. No believer in partial methods, he had a simple but powerful appeal:

> *If you really will, you surely can.*
> *But you never can unless you will.*

He formulated a simple pledge that was framed on a broad cross for abstainers to proclaim:

I promise to abstain from all intoxicating drinks except used medicinally and by order of a medical man, and to discountenance the cause and practice of intemperance.

As a result, thousands of pubs closed and coffee shops appeared on every street corner. Matthew's campaign took him to America in 1849, where he was welcomed by President Zachary Taylor. Over 600,000 people took the pledge as Matthew visited Boston, Philadelphia, Cincinnati, Little Rock, New Orleans, Florida, Georgia, Tennessee, Virginia and Delaware.

TEN PLAGUES UPON EGYPT

Then the Lord said to Moses, 'See, I have made you like God to Pharaoh, and your brother Aaron will be your prophet. You are to say everything I command you, and your brother Aaron is to tell Pharaoh to let the Israelites go out of his country. But I will harden Pharaoh's heart, and though I multiply my miraculous signs and wonders in Egypt, he will not listen to you. Then I will lay my hand on Egypt and with mighty acts of judgment I will bring out my divisions, my people the Israelites. And the Egyptians will know that I am the Lord when I stretch out my hand against Egypt and bring the Israelites out of it.'
Exodus 7:1–5

1. Blood	2. Frogs	3. Gnats
4. Flies	5. Livestock	6. Boils
7. Hail	8. Locusts	9. Darkness
	10. Firstborn	

NINE GIFTS AND NINE FRUITS OF THE HOLY SPIRIT

Now to each one the manifestation of the Spirit is given for the common good. To one there is given through the Spirit the message of **wisdom**, to another the message of **knowledge** by means of the same Spirit, to another **faith** by the same Spirit, to another gifts of **healing** by that one Spirit, to another **miraculous powers**, to another **prophecy**, to another **distinguishing between spirits**, to another **speaking in different kinds of tongues**, and to still another **the interpretation of tongues**. All these are the work of one and the same Spirit, and he gives them to each one, just as he determines.
1 Corinthians 12:7–11

But the fruit of the Spirit is **love, joy, peace, patience, kindness, goodness, faithfulness, gentleness** and **self-control**. Against such things there is no law.
Galatians 5:22–23

JOHN 3:16 – THE PINNACLE

Probably the most popular verse in the Bible is John 3:16. Here's why:

GOD	the greatest lover
SO LOVED	in the greatest degree
THE WORLD	to the greatest number
THAT HE GAVE	with the greatest act
HIS ONLY BEGOTTEN SON	by the greatest gift
THAT WHOSOEVER	through the greatest offer
BELIEVETH	in the greatest simplicity
IN HIM	from the greatest man
SHOULD NOT PERISH	by the greatest promise
BUT	with the greatest difference
HAVE	to the greatest certainty
ETERNAL LIFE	for the greatest future

CHECK OUT YOUR VICAR'S VESTMENTS

Clerical attire gives a good indication of the type of church a priest leads – the more traditional the garb, the more traditional the church. The technical term for clerical gear is 'vestments', and here are some vestments still to be seen on clerical bodies today:

Chasuble: a seamless outer cloak worn during communion.

Maniple: worn during communion, this is a strip worn over the left wrist. It relates to the cloth Jesus may have used to clean the feet of his disciples.

Pallium: a strip of white wool with six embedded crosses running across the shoulders.

Stole: a long scarf worn around the neck or over one arm. Worn during communion, it symbolizes humility.

Alb: an all-in-one tunic that symbolizes purity.

Cassock: the black dress of an ordinary priest. Ideally, it should have 33 front buttons to signify Jesus' 33 years on earth. In the Catholic Church, bishops wear purple, cardinals red and the pope white.

WILLIAM CAREY – FROM COBBLER TO MISSIONARY TO INDIA

Expect great things from God.
Attempt great things for God.

A truly great servant of God, William Carey was born in 1761 in an obscure English village. He overcame many obstacles to take the gospel to India. Here are a few brief highlights:

❏ As a cobbler in the village of Moulton, Northamptonshire, Carey heard the missionary call. According to his diary, his attention to missions was first awakened by reading the *Last Voyage of Captain Cook*.

❏ He mastered Latin, Greek, Hebrew and Italian in preparation for mission.

❏ He fashioned a leather globe of the world and prayed, *'Here am I; send me!'*

❏ He published his masterpiece, *Enquiry into the Obligations of the Christians to Use Means for the Conversion of the Heathen*.

❏ In 1792, he preached on 'Expect great things from God. Attempt great things for God' in Nottingham, England. He also set up the Baptist Missionary Society.

❏ In 1793, he arrived in Hooghly, India, but saw no converts for seven years.

❏ By the time of his death in 1834, Carey had led hundreds to Christ, founded a Christian college at Serampore, translated the Bible into 40 languages (including Sanskrit, Bengali and Hindustani) and seen an end to the heathen practice of *suttee* (the burning of widows on their husbands' funeral pyres).

STATIONS OF THE CROSS

Christian pilgrims visiting Jerusalem often followed in the footsteps of Christ, tracing his path to the cross. The Catholic Church recognized this practice as a good way of identifying with the passion of Christ, and in the Middle Ages many European towns and cities enacted 'stations of the cross' ceremonies. Eventually, 14 (or 15 including the resurrection) stations or 'milestones' were recognized, and these are:

1. Jesus is condemned to die.

2. Jesus accepts his cross.

3. Jesus falls for the first time.

4. Jesus meets his mother.

5. Simon helps carry the cross.

6. Veronica wipes the face of Jesus.

7. Jesus falls for the second time.

8. Jesus speaks to the women.

9. Jesus falls for the third time.

10. Jesus is stripped of his garments.

11. Jesus is nailed to the cross.

12. Jesus dies on the cross.

13. Jesus is taken down from the cross.

14. Jesus is laid in the tomb.

15. Jesus is resurrected.

PSALMS OF ASCENT

The psalms of Ascent are Psalms 120–134 in the Bible. They may have been sung by pilgrims three times a year while on their way to Jerusalem to celebrate the major festivals. Each psalm draws closer to the pilgrims' heavenly vision from initial sight to dedication and finally reaching Mount Zion.

AUGUSTUS TOPLADY (1740–77)

Little is known about this hymn-writer and poet but many will be familiar with his most famous hymn, 'Rock of Ages'. This is one of his many entreaties for the rejection of Arminianism, the belief that God has given man the choice to accept or reject him:

WHAT WILL BE YOUR SONG?

What do you think your song will be when you come to heaven? Blessed be God, that he gave me free will; and blessed be my own dear self, that I made a good use of it? O no, no! Such a song as that was never heard in heaven yet, nor ever will be, while God is God, and heaven is heaven.

Look into the book of Revelation, and there you will find the employ of the blessed, and the strains which they sing. They cast their crowns before the throne, saying, 'Thou art worthy, for thou wast slain, and hast redeemed us to God by thy blood, out of every kindred and tongue and people and nation' (Revelation 4:10). There is discriminating grace for you! 'Thou hast redeemed us out of every kindred,' that is, from the rest of mankind. Is not this particular election and limited redemption?

The church below may be liable to err, and if any visible church upon earth pretends to be infallible, the very pretension itself demonstrates that she is not so. But there is a church which I will venture to pronounce infallible. And what church is that? The church of the glorified, who shine as stars at God's right hand. And, upon the infallible testimony of that infallible church, a testimony recorded in the infallible pages of inspiration, I will venture to assert that not one grain of Arminianism ever attended a saint into heaven.

THE SEVEN CHURCHES OF REVELATION

The church in Ephesus:	'I know thy works, and thy labour, and thy patience' (2:2)
The church in Smyrna:	'I know thy works, and tribulation, and poverty' (2:9)
The church in Pergamum:	'I know thy works and where thou dwellest' (2:13)
The church in Thyatira:	'I know thy works, and charity, and service, and faith' (2:19)
The church in Sardis:	'I know thy works, that thou hast a name that thou livest' (3:1)
The church in Philadelphia:	'I know thy works: behold, I have set before thee an open door' (3:8)
The church in Laodicea:	'I know thy works, that thou art neither cold nor hot' (3:16)

SNAKE HANDLERS

Mark 16:18 states, 'They will pick up snakes with their hands; and when they drink deadly poison, it will not hurt them at all; they will place their hands on sick people, and they will get well.'

Although not an invitation to grab the nearest snake, George Went Hensley, also known as 'Little George,' took this verse literally. From 1910 for over a decade, Little George carried a live rattlesnake wherever he preached, He went on to start the Church of Jesus With Signs Following. Travelling across the hills of Grasshopper Valley in Tennessee, he would challenge congregations to grab the snake as an affirmation of their faith. All went well, until, inevitably, one of the faithful died of a snakebite.

However, Little George's antics spread throughout the hills of Kentucky. By the early 1940s, around 2,500 snake handlers were imitating him across the states of Florida, Georgia, Alabama, North and South Carolina, Virginia, West Virginia, Ohio and Texas. The movement would have grown even more if state legislatures, alarmed at the rising number of deaths from snakebites in churches, had not passed laws forbidding snakes in church.

MALACHY AND THE LAST TEN POPES

Malachy O'Morgair, born in 1094 in Armagh in Ireland, was the first Irish saint to be canonized by Pope Clement III in 1190. Malachy was a noted mystic, miracle worker and healer. He also claimed to be a prophet, and in 1139, he claimed to have received a vision showing him all the popes from his time until the end of the world. According to his prophecies, after John Paul II, there will be only two more popes before the end!

PROPHECY	POPE
The burning fire	Pius X (1903–140
Religion laid waste	Benedict XV (1914–22)
Unshaken faith	Pius XI (1922–39)
An angelic shepherd	Pius XII (1939–58)
Pastor and mariner	John XXIII (1958–63)
Flower of flowers	Paul VI (1963–78)
The half moon	John Paul I (1978–78)
The labour of the son	John Paul II (1978–present)
The glory of the olive	*From the Order of St Benedict*
Peter the Roman	*Satan taking the form of a man*

THE LORD'S PRAYER IN VARIOUS LANGUAGES

ENGLISH

Our Father, who art in heaven, hallowed be Thy name. Thy kingdom come. Thy will be done on earth as it is in heaven. Give us this day our daily bread and forgive us our trespasses as we forgive those who trespass against us. And lead us not into temptation, but deliver us from evil. Amen.

AFRIKAANS

Onse Vader wat in die hemel is, laat U naam geheilig word, laat U koningkryk kom, laat U wil geskiet, op aarde, so ook in die hemel. Gee ons vandag ons daaglikse brood, en vergeef ons ons skulde soos ons ook ons skuldenaars vergewe. En lei ons nie in versoeking nie, maar verlos ons van die bose. Want aan U behoort die krag en die heerlikheid tot in ewigheid. Amen.

CATALAN

Pare nostra del cel, sigui santificat el teu nom; vingui el teu Regne; faci's la teva voluntat, com al cel, així també a la terra. Dóna'ns avui el nostre pa de cada dia; i perdona'ns les nostres ofenses, com també nosaltres hem perdonat els qui ens ofenen; i no deixis que caiguem en la temptació, ans deslliura'ns del Maligne.

DUTCH

Onze Vader, die in de hemelen zijt, geheiligd zij Uw naam. Uw rijk kome. Uw wil geschiede op aarde als in de hemel. Geef ons heden ons dagelijks brood, en vergeef ons onze schulden, gelijk ook wij vergeven aan onze schuldenaren. En leid ons niet in bekoring, maar verlos ons van het kwade.

ESTONIAN

Meie Isa, kes Sa oled taevas, pühitsetud saagu Sinu nimi. Sinu riik tulgu. Sinu tahtmine sündigu kui taevas nõnda ka maa peal. Meie igapäevane leib anna meile tänapäev. Ja anna andeks meile meie võlad, kui ka meie andeks anname oma võlglastele. Ja ära saada meid mitte kiusatuse sisse, vaid päästa meid ära kurjast: sest Sinu päralt on riik, ja vägi, ja au igavesti, Aamen.

FIJIAN

Tama i keimami mai lomalagi, Me vakarokorokotaki ma yacamuni. Me yaco na nomuni lewa. Me caka na lomamuni e vuravura me vaka sa caka mai lomalagi. Solia mai vei keimami e na na siga oqo na kakana e yaga vei keimami. Ia kakua ni cudruvi keikami e na vuku ni neimami valvala ca, me vaka keimami sa sega ni cudruvi ira era sai valavala ca vei keimami. Ia kakua ni kauti keimami ki na vere, ka mo ni vakabulai keimami mai na ca: Ni sa nomuni na lewa, kei na kaukauwa, kei na vakarokoroko, ka sega ni mudu. Emeni.

HEBREW

Avinu shebashamayim yitkadesh shimcha, tavo malchutecha, yease retsoncha kebashamayim ken ba'aretz. Et lechem chukenu ten lanu hayom, uslach lanu al chataeinu, kefi shesolchim gam anachnu lachot'im lanu. Veal tevienu lijdei nisajon ki im chaltzenu min hara. Ki lecha hamamlacha hagvura vehatif'eret leolmei olamim. Amen.

Japanese

Ten ni imasu watashitachi no chichi yo O-na ga agameraremasu yoo ni O-kuni ga kimasu yoo ni Mikokoro ga ten de okonawareru yoo ni Chi de mo konawaremasu yoo ni Watashitachi no higoto no kate o kyoo mo o-atae kudasai Watashitachi no oime o o-yurushi kudasai Watashitachi mo watashitachi ni oime no aru hitotachi o yurushimashita Watashitachi o kokoromi ni awasenaide, aku kara o-sukui kudasai Kuni to chikara to sakae wa tokoshie ni anata no mono da kara desu Aamen.

Latin

Pater noster, qui es in caelis, sanctificetur nomen tuum. Adveniat regnum tuum. Fiat voluntas tua, sicut in caelo et in terra. Panem nostrum quotidianum da nobis hodie, et dimitte nobis debita nostra sicut et nos dimittimus debitoribus nostris. Et ne nos inducas in tentationem, sed libera nos a malo. Amen.

From a thirteenth-century manuscript in the library of Caius College, Cambridge

Fader oure that art in heve, i-halgeed be thi nome, i-cume thi kinereiche, y-worthe thi wylle also is in hevene so be an erthe, oure iche-dayes-bred ʒif us today, and forʒif us our gultes, also we forʒifet oure gultare, and ne led ows nowth into fondingge, auth ales ows of harme. So be it.

From a fourteenth-century manuscript, in the library of St. John's college, Cambridge

Fader oure that art in heuene, halewed be thi name: come thi kyngdom: fulfild be thi wil in heuene as in erthe: oure ech day bred ʒef vs to day, and forʒeue vs oure dettes as we forʒeueth to oure detoures: and ne led vs nouʒ in temptacion, bote deliuere vs of euel. So be it.

From a fifteenth-century manuscript in the Bodleian library, Oxford

Fader oure that art in heuene, halewed be thy name: thy kyngedom come to thee: thy wille be do in erthe as in heuen: oure eche dayes brede ʒeue us to daye: and forʒeue us oure dettes as we forʒeue to oure dettoures: and lede us noʒte into temptacion: bot delyver us from yvel. Amen.

FROM AN ENGLISH AND LATIN PRYMER, PARIS (1538)
Our father whiche art in heuen, halowed be thy name. Let thy kingdome cum unto us. Thy wyll be fulfylled as well in erthe, as it is in heuen. Gyue vs this daye our daylye breade. And forgyue us our trespasses, as we forgyue them that trespas agaynst vs. And lede vs nat in to temtacyon. But delyuer vs from euyll. So be it.

CLASSES OF ANGELS

In 1886, Earnest A. Wallis Budge, M.A., attempted a classification of angels in his classic text, *The Book of the Bee*. A summary of his classification: 'The number of each one of these classes of angels is equal to the number of all mankind from Adam to the resurrection.'

UPPER ORDER

Cherubim: priests (*kumrê*)

Seraphim: chief priests

Throne: bearers of God's throne

MIDDLE ORDER

Lord: government of powers and rulers

Power: to direct Christians to victory

Ruler: have power over spiritual treasures

LOWER ORDER

Principalities: to direct weather

Archangel: to direct animals

Angel: to direct man (as in 'guardian' angels)

THE SOCIETY OF FRIENDS (QUAKERS)

ADVICE ON SCRIPTURES OF THE OLD AND NEW TESTAMENTS

We tenderly and earnestly advise and exhort all parents and heads of families, that they endeavour to instruct their children and families in the doctrines and precepts of the Christian religion, as contained in the scriptures; and that they excite them to the diligent reading of those excellent writings, which plainly set forth the miraculous conception, birth, holy life, wonderful

works, blessed example, meritorious death, and glorious
resurrection, ascension and mediation of our Lord and Saviour
Jesus Christ; and to educate their children in the belief of those
important truths, as well as in the belief of the inward
manifestation and operation of the Holy Spirit on their own
minds, that they may reap the benefit and advantage thereof, for
their own peace and everlasting happiness; which is infinitely
preferable to all other considerations.

Anon 1732

COMMUNION

A little red wine,
kenotic memories,
   a Spanish Renaissance
   still-life of platters and
       wholemeal bread, where
         umber night's messianic-
               thief communes with
                 his chosen few at the
                     appointed angelic hour.
                       designated space-room,
                         where midsummer
                           is raptured and
                           millennial, as I
                       carry out his gift like
                   a midsummer-night's
             lutenist under this
         risen sky, this
     tone painted
robe of my
Humanitas.

Mark Wilson

PRAYER OF EXORCISM

Priest: I exorcise thee, every unclean spirit, in the name of God (X) the Father Almighty, and in the name of Jesus (X) Christ, His Son, our Lord and Judge, and in the power of the Holy Spirit, that thou depart from this creature of God, (persons' name) which our Lord hath designed to call unto His holy temple, that it may be made the temple of the living God, and that the Holy Spirit (X) may dwell therein. Through the same Christ our Lord, who shall come to judge the living and the dead, and the world by fire.

Person: Amen.

X = Sign of the Cross
(Ref: Catholic Church Sacrament of Baptism of the Manual of Prayers, 1889.)

FAMOUS SPORTING CHRISTIANS

Carl Lewis	Athletics	Michelle Akers	Football
Kris Akabusi	Athletics	Cyrille Regis	Football
Jonathan Edwards	Athletics	Bert Konterman	Football
Eric Liddell	Athletics	Gavin Peacock	Football
Stephanie Cook	Athletics	Bernhard Langer	Golf
Ato Boldon	Athletics	Paul Azinger	Golf
Maurice Green	Athletics	Tom Lehman	Golf
Jon Drummon	Athletics	Va'aiga Tuigamala	Rugby Union
Jackie Joyner-Kersee	Athletics	Jonah Lomu	Rugby Union
George Foreman	Boxing	Apollo Perelini	Rugby Union
Evander Holyfield	Boxing	John Naber	Swimming
Meadowlark Lemmon	Basketball	Josh Davis	Swimming
Charles Thomas Stud	Cricket	Michael Chang	Tennis
David Shepherd	Cricket		

THE LANGUAGE OF JESUS

Jesus probably spoke in Aramaic (also known as Syriac, Assyrian and Chaldean), a language that was very widespread in his day. Although the Gospels are written in Greek, some of the original Aramaic words of Jesus have been preserved. Here are some examples:

His cry from the cross is quoted in the original Aramaic in Matthew 27:46:
'Eloi, Eloi, lama sabachthani?' ('My God, my God, why have you forsaken me?')

In Mark 5:41, he addresses the young girl, saying:
'Talitha koum!' ('Little girl, get up!')

In Mark 7:34, he says:
'Ephphatha!' ('Be opened!')

In Mark 14:36 Jesus uses a familiar, childlike word to talk to God:
'Abba' ('Father')

CHRISTIANITY IN INDIA

It is estimated that there are over 25 million Christians in India, concentrated in the regions of Kerala, Goa and Misoram. Over three quarters are Catholic. Tradition has it that the apostle Thomas came to India in AD 52 and landed at Kodungallur on the Keralan coast. He preached the gospel to the Brahmin families of Kerala, many of whom received the faith. He established seven Churches there: Kodungallur, Kottakkavu, Palayur, Kollam, Kokkamangalam, Niranam and Chayil.

Twenty years later, Thomas was martyred in Madras and buried there. As well as Catholic Thomas Christians, there are also non-Catholic Thomas Christians: the Jacobites, the Anjoorians, the Anglicans, the Marthomites, or Nestorians, and the St Thomas Evangelical Church of India. Altogether, there are around six million non-Catholics in India, including Orthodox Christian Protestants.

BIBLE TRANSLATIONS INTO ENGLISH

DATE	TRANSLATOR/TRANSLATION	COMMENTS
1380	John Wycliffe	From Latin Vulgate
1525	William Tyndale's New Testament	Many copies destroyed by Cuthbert Tunstall (Bishop of London)
1530	William Tyndale	Tyndale's Pentateuch published
1535	Miles Coverdale	From Zürich Bible under the patronage of Thomas Cromwell. First version of the whole Bible in English
1537	Matthew's Bible	From Tyndale's Pentateuch and Coverdale's New Testament
1539	The Great Bible	Authorized by King Henry VIII; also known as Cranmer's Bible
1539	The Taverner's Bible	A 'pirated' edition of Matthew's Bible
1560	The Geneva Bible	Translator unknown, but Miles Coverdale and John Know may have been involved
1568	The Bishop's Bible	The second authorized Bible after the Great Bible
1582	The Rheims-Douai Bible	The basis for all English Catholic versions of the Bible. The work was undertaken by members of the English College at Douai in Flanders
1611	Authorized Version (King James Version)	Translated by order of King James I, by 47 scholars from Cambridge (Genesis to 1 Chronicles), London (2 Chronicles to the Apocrypha) and Oxford (Prophets, Gospels, Acts and Revelation). Revised in 1629, 1638, 1762 and 1769
1881	English Revised Version	From the Convocation of the Province of Canterbury (February 1870). New Testament published in 1881, followed by the Old Testament in 1885

DATE	TRANSLATOR/TRANSLATION	COMMENTS
1901	American Standard Version	Revised version of the Authorized Version
1952	New Revised Standard Version	The work of 22 scholars
1966	Today's English Version (The Good New Bible)	A new translation in standard, everyday English
1966	Jerusalem Bible	Based on two principles, *aggiornamento* (keeping abreast of the times) and *approfondimentor* (deepening of theological thought)
1970	New English Bible	A 'free' translation
1971	The Living Bible	Paraphrase by one author, Kenneth Taylor
1971	New American Standard Bible	The work of 58 scholars
1974	Revised English Bible	Produced by the Joint Committee of the Churches
1978	New International Version	The work of over 100 scholars
1982	The New King James Version	The work of over 130 scholars
1982	The New Jerusalem Bible	Revision of the Jerusalem Bible
1988	The Word Made Fresh	Paraphrase by Andy Edington, President Emeritus of Schreiner Junior College and High School, Texas
1992	Contemporary English Version	The work of over 40 scholars
2000	International Standard Version	An attempt to produce a readable and accurate English translation for the twenty-first century

SOME CHRISTIAN DOCTRINES

Bibliology (the word of God) – 2 Timothy 3:16

Theology (God) – Deuteronomy 4:6; Ephesians 4:6

Christology (Christ the Son) – John 1:1–2, 14

Pneumatology (the Holy Spirit) – John 16:7–11

Angelology (angels) – 2 Peter 2:4

Anthropology (man) – Genesis 1:26–27

Hamartialogy (sin) – Romans 5:12

Soteriology (salvation) – John 3:16

Ecclesiology (the Church) – Ephesians 4:11–16.

Eschatology (end-times) – 1 Thessalonians 4:13–18

FORBIDDEN MARRIAGE PARTNERS

According to the Anglican Church, 'kindred and affinity are forbidden to marry together'. Thus a man may not marry his:

1. Mother
2. Daughter
3. Father's mother
4. Mother's mother
5. Son's daughter
6. Daughter's daughter
7. Sister
8. Father's daughter
9. Mother's daughter
10. Wife's mother
11. Wife's daughter
12. Father's wife
13. Son's wife
14. Father's father's wife
15. Mother's father's wife
16. Wife's father's mother
17. Wife's mother's mother
18. Wife's son's daughter
19. Wife's daughter's daughter
20. Son's son's wife
21. Daughter's son's wife
22. Father's sister
23. Mother's sister
24. Brother's daughter
25. Sister's daughter

Similarly, a woman may not marry her father, son, father's father, and so on.

SEVEN WORDS FROM THE CROSS

The proclamations of Jesus:
1. 'Father, forgive them, for they know not what they do' (Luke 23:34).
2. 'Today shalt thou be with me in paradise' (Luke 23:43).
3. 'Woman, behold thy son' (John 19:26).
4. 'My God, my God, why hast thou forsaken me?' (Matthew 27:46).
5. 'I thirst' (John 19:28).
6. 'It is finished' (John 19:30).
7. 'Father, into thy hands I commend my spirit' (Luke 23:46).

SOME CHRISTIAN MUSIC FESTIVALS

These include:

Cornerstone Festival (USA) – Illinois

Parachute Noise, Worship and Music (New Zealand) – Auckland

Proud to Be Catholic (USA)

Atlanta Fest (USA)

Icthus Festival (USA)

Fishermen's Festival (USA)

Spirit Fest MidWest (USA)

Spirit West Coast (USA) – California

Agape Music Festival (USA) – Illinois

Creation (USA) – Pennsylvania and Washington

Flevo Festival (Netherlands) – Driebergen

Alive (USA) – Ohio

Greenbelt (UK) – Cheltenham

Sonshine (USA) – Montana

SonFest (USA) – Florida

MOVABLE FEASTS

Movable feast are so named because they vary according to the date of Easter Day. In the Anglican Church, the movable feasts are calculated thus:

Number of weeks before Easter Day	Movable feast
Nine	Septuagesima
Eight	Sexagesima
Seven	Quinquagesima
Six	Quadragesima
Number of weeks after Easter Day	**Movable feast**
Five	Rogation
Forty days	Ascension
Seven	Whit
Eight	Trinity

Advent Sunday is always the *nearest* Sunday to the Feast of St Andrew, whether before it or after it.

DENUNCIATION OF GOD'S ANGER AND JUDGMENT AGAINST SINNERS

A commination used by the Anglican Church on the first day of Lent:

Minister: Cursed is the man that maketh any carved or molten image, to worship it.

And the people shall answer and say, Amen.

Minister: Cursed is he that curseth his father or mother.
Answer: Amen

Minister: Cursed is he that removeth his neighbour's landmark.
Answer: Amen

Minister: Cursed is he that maketh the blind to go out of his way.
Answer: Amen

Minister: Cursed is he that perverteth the judgment of the stranger, the fatherless and the widow.
Answer: Amen

Minister: Cursed is he that smiteth his neighbour secretly.
Answer: Amen

Minister: Cursed is he that lieth with his neighbour's wife.
Answer: Amen

Minister: Cursed is he that taketh reward to slay the innocent.
Answer: Amen

Minister: Cursed is he that putteth his trust in man and taketh man for defence, and his heart goeth from the Lord.
Answer: Amen

Minister: Cursed are the unmerciful, fornicators and adulterers, coveteous persons, idolaters, slanderers, drunkards and extortionists.
Answer: Amen

The Book of Common Prayer

LITANY OF FOUR LAST THINGS *(edited)*

DEATH
We are dying day by day,
Soon from earth we pass away;
Lord of Life, to Thee we pray:
Hear us, holy Jesu.

Ere we hear the angel's call,
And the shadows round us fall,
Be our Saviour, be our all;
Hear us, holy Jesu

JUDGMENT

When Thy summons we obey
On the dreadful Judgment Day,
Let not fear our souls dismay,
Hear us, holy Jesu.

While the lost in terror fly,
May we see with joyful eye
Our redemption drawing nigh:
Hear us, holy Jesu.

HELL

From the awful place of doom,
Where in rayless outer gloom
Dead souls lie as in a tomb,
Save us, holy Jesu.

From the black, the dull despair
Ruined men and angels share,
From the dread companions there,
Save us, holy Jesu.

HEAVEN

Where Thy saints in glory reign,
Free from sorrow, free from pain,
Pure from every guilty stain,
Bring us, holy Jesu.

Where the captives find release,
Where all foes from troubling cease,
Where the weary rest in peace,
Bring us, holy Jesu.

The Book of Common Prayer

THE URIM AND THE THUMMIM

Also put the Urim and the Thummim in the breastpiece, so they
may be over Aaron's heart whenever he enters the presence of the
Lord. Thus Aaron will always bear the means of making
decisions for the Israelites over his heart before the Lord.
Exodus 28:30

It is not definitively known what Urim and Thummim were, but they
were used by the High Priest, Aaron, and his successors to 'enquire of
the mind of the Lord'. Urim means something like 'lights' in Hebrew
and Thummim means something like 'perfections'. Thus it could be
argued that the use of these devices gave light and revealed the perfect
will of God. Urim and Thummim were part of Aaron's attire, worn as
'the breastpiece of judgment' close to the heart. The Roman historian
Josephus adds that they were 'two sardonyx buttons, worn on the
shoulders' that emitted luminous rays to indicate a favourable
response. The precise mode of operation is lost in antiquity.

SEVEN 'I AMS' OF JESUS

In St John's Gospel, Jesus makes seven declarations beginning with the
phrase 'I am…' This signifies his deity, since the phrase recalls the
story of Moses. When Moses asked God who he should say had sent
him, God revealed himself as, 'I am who I am' (Exodus 3:14)

I AM…

The light of the World (John 8:12)

The gate (John 10:7)

The good shepherd (John 10:11)

The resurrection and the life (John 11:25)

The way, the truth and the life (John 14:6)

The true vine (John 15:1)

He (Jesus of Nazareth) (John 18:5)

MNEMONIC

Def: **mne·mon·ic**: *adj.*— assisting or intended to assist memory.

ENTERING THE PROMISED LAND
Only Joshua son of Nun
And Caleb son of Jephunneh,
Entered the land of milk and honey.

REMEMBERING THE NAMES OF THE TWELVE DISCIPLES

This is the way the disciples run:
Peter, Andrew, James and John,
Phillip and Bartholomew, Thomas next,
Matthew, and then James the less,
Judas the greater, Simon the zealot
And finally, Judas the traitor.

THE TEN COMMANDMENTS IN RHYME

1. Thou no gods shalt have before me

2. Before no idol bend the knee.

3. Take not the name of God in vain.

4. Do not the Sabbath day profane.

5. Give thy parents honour due.

6. Take heed that thou no murder do.

7. Abstain from words and deeds unclean.

8. Steal not, for thou by God art seen.

9. Tell not a wilful lie, nor love it.

10. What is thy neighbour's do not covet.

REMEMBERING THE PENTATEUCHAL BOOKS OF THE BIBLE
General **E**lectric **L**ights **N**ever **D**im (Genesis, Exodus, Leviticus, Numbers, Deuteronomy)

Definition of Grace:	Definition of Faith:
God's	**F**orsaking
Riches	**A**ll
At	**I**
Christ's	**T**rust
Expense	**H**im

SEVEN DEADLY SINS, HEAVENLY VIRTUES AND CORPORAL WORKS OF MERCY

Deadly Sins	Heavenly Virtues	Corporal Works of Mercy
Pride	Faith	Feeding the hungry
Envy	Hope	Giving drink to the thirsty
Gluttony	Charity	Giving shelter to strangers
Lust	Fortitude	Clothing the naked
Anger	Justice	Visiting the sick
Greed	Temperance	Ministering to prisoners
Sloth	Prudence	Burying the dead

'I FELT MY HEART STRANGELY WARMED'

Extract from John Wesley's account of his conversion on 24 May 1738:

In the evening I went very unwillingly to a society in Aldersgate Street, where one was reading Luther's preface to the Epistle to the Romans. About a quarter before nine, while he was describing the change which God works in the heart through faith in Christ, I felt my heart strangely warmed. I felt I did trust in Christ, Christ alone, for salvation; and an assurance was given me that he had taken away my sins, even mine, and saved me from the law of sin and death.

I began to pray with all my might for those who had in a more especial manner despitefully used me and persecuted me. I then testified openly to all there what I now first felt in my heart. But it was not long before the enemy suggested, 'This cannot be faith; for where is thy joy?' Then was I taught that peace and victory over sin are essential to faith in the Captain of our salvation...

THIRTY OBSOLETE WORDS IN THE AUTHORIZED VERSION OR KING JAMES BIBLE

OBSOLETE WORD	REFERENCE	MEANING
1. Ambassage	Luke 14:32	Message
2. Asswage	Genesis 8:1	To subside
3. Bewray	Matthew 26:73	To expose
4. Calamus	Exodus 30:23	Reed
5. Cankerworm	Joel 1:4	Caterpillar
6. Caul	Hosea 13:8	Membrane around the heart
7. Cockatrice	Isaiah 11:8	Serpent
8. Collops	Job 15:27	Slices of meat
9. Countervail	Esther 7:4	Compensate
10. Daysman	Job 9:33	Umpire, referee
11. Draught House	2 Kings 10:27	Privy
12. Emerods	1 Samuel 5:6	Piles
13. Evilfavouredness	Deuteronomy 17:1	Ugliness
14. Goodman	Matthew 20:11	Master of the house
15. Habergeon	Job 41:26	Coat of mail
16. Husbandman	Genesis 9:20	Farmer
17. Implead	Acts 19:38	Accuse
18. Indite	Psalm 45:1	Compose
19. Jacinth	Revelation 9:17	Hyacinth
20. Ligure	Exodus 28:19	Precious stone
21. Murrain	Exodus 9:3	Cattle plague
22. Ossifrage	Leviticus 11:13	Bearded vulture
23. Palmerworm	Joel 1:4	Caterpillar
24. Potsherd	Psalm 22:15	Broken pottery
25. Pygarg	Deuteronomy 14:5	Antelope
26. Quaternion	Acts 12:4	A party of four men

27. Scall	Leviticus 13:30	Skin lesion
28. Undersetters	1 Kings 7:30	Supports
29. Winebibber	Matthew 11:19	Drunkard
30. Yokefellow	Philippians 4:3	Fellow worker

'THE OLDER WILL SERVE THE YOUNGER...' (GENESIS 25:13)

It is a scriptural principle that God's choice does not necessarily accord with ours. Thus:

> Isaac was blessed above Ishmael.
>
> Jacob was blessed above Esau.
>
> Perez was blessed above Zerah.
>
> Joseph was blessed above his older brothers.
>
> Ephraim was blessed above Mannaseh.
>
> Judah was blessed above Reuben.
>
> Gideon was blessed above his older brothers.
>
> David was blessed above his older brothers.

FUNNY CHURCH NOTICES

Worm welcome to all who have come today.

Don't miss this Saturday's exhibit by Christian Martian Arts.

We have received word of the sudden passing of Reverend Smith this morning during the worship service. Now let's sing 'Praise God from Whom All Blessings Flow'.

Next Friday we will be serving hot gods for lunch.

If you would like to make a donation, fill out a form, enclose a cheque and drip in the collection basket.

Applications are now being accepted for two year-old nursery workers.

We are grateful for the help of those who cleaned up the grounds around the church building and the rector.

Newsletters are not being sent to absentees because of their weight.

Sign-up sheet for anyone wishing to be water baptized on the table in the foyer.

Helpers are needed! Please sign up on the information sheep.

Thank you dead friends.

Diana and Don request your presents at their wedding.

Lent is that period for preparing for Holy Weed and Easter.

Bless the Lord, O my soul, and forget all his benefits.

WATCHES OF THE NIGHT AND DAY

'And there was evening and there was morning – the first day' (Genesis 1:5).

The Jewish civil day differed from the natural day (sunrise to sunrise) because it was reckoned from sunset to sunset.

OLD TESTAMENT WATCHES OF THE NIGHT

First – sunset till midnight

Middle – midnight till 3 am

Morning – 3 am till 6 am

OLD TESTAMENT WATCHES OF THE DAY

Morning – 6 am till 10 am

Heat of the day – 10 am till 2 pm

Cool of the day – 2 pm till 6 pm

NEW TESTAMENT WATCHES OF THE NIGHT

First watch (evening) – 6 pm till 9 pm

Second watch (midnight) – 9 pm till 12 midnight

Third watch (Cock crow) – 12 midnight till 3 am

Fourth watch (morning) – 3 am till 6 am

NEW TESTAMENT WATCHES OF THE DAY

Third hour – 6 am till 9 am

Sixth hour – 9 am till 12 noon

Ninth hour – 12 noon till 3 pm

Twelfth hour – 3 pm till 6 pm

EARLY CHRISTIAN HERESIES

A heresy may be defined as a deviation from the orthodox teachings of a faith. Christianity has endured many heresies over the centuries. Most heresies centred around the person of Jesus, his divinity, his humanity and his teachings. The table below lists some of them:

HERESY	EXPLANATION
Adoptionism	Christ was not divine until he was baptized
Apollinarism	Christ not fully divine or fully human
Arianism	Denial of the Trinity
Docetism	Christ did not have a physical body
Donatism	Rejected believers who renounced their faith during persecution
Gnosticism	Secret, special knowledge available only to a few
Jansenism	Overemphasis of predestination
Monophysitism	Christ had only one nature
Nestorianism	Christ was two persons, one human, the other divine
Patripassianism	God the Father, not Jesus, suffered on the cross
Pelagianism	The sin of Adam and Eve did not corrupt human nature
Psilanthropism or Socianism	Denial of the divine nature of Christ

ICHTHUS

 The Greek word for fish, Ichthus, is used to symbolize the Saviour, Jesus Christ. It was used in this way from the first century, after the time of the apostles.

The fish symbol was a rebus, an enigmatic pictorial representation of a word, that allowed early Christians to identify one another, especially in times of persecution. When scrawled on a wall, or on the ground in the marketplace, or near a fountain where people congregated, it let wandering Christians know that others of their faith had come to this community.

i-ch-th-u-s = **I**esous **Ch**ristos **Th**eou **U**ios **S**orter (Jesus Christ, God's Son, Saviour)

A JESUS FOR ALL NATIONS

Jesus was Jewish because:
1. He went into his father's business.
2. He lived at home until the age of 30.
3. He was sure his mother was a virgin, and his mother was sure he was God.

Jesus was English because:
1. He had good manners.
2. He loved the seaside.
3. He didn't mind being caught out in a storm.

Jesus was Australian because:
1. He liked eating outdoors.
2. He liked the beach.
3. He liked going to solitary places.

Jesus was Swiss because:
1. He liked climbing mountains.
2. He loved being beside lakes.
3. He was always on time.

Jesus was French because:
1. He loved good food.

2. He loved good wine.
3. He loved a good debate.

Jesus was Californian because:
    1. He never cut his hair.
    2. He walked around barefoot.
    3. He invented a new religion.

NEW TESTAMENT CATECHISM

Matthew and **Mark** and **Luke** and **John** the holy Gospels wrote,
Describing how the Saviour died – his life and what he taught.
Acts proves how God the apostles owned with signs in every place.
St Paul in **Romans** teaches us how man is saved by grace.
Th'apostle in **Corinthians** instructs, exhorts, reproves;
Galatians shows that faith in Christ alone, the Father loves.
Ephesians and **Philippians** tell what Christians ought to be.
Colossians bids us live to God and for eternity,
In **Thessalonians** we are taught the Lord will come from heaven.
In **Timothy** and **Titus** a bishop's rule is given.
Philemon marks a Christian's love which only Christians know.
Hebrews reveals the Gospel as prefigured by the Law.
St James insists that without deeds faith is but vain and dead:
And **Peter** points the narrow way in which the saints are led.
St John in his epistles on love delights to dwell,
And **Jude** gives awful warning of judgment, wrath and hell.
The **Revelation** prophesies of that tremendous day
When Christ, and Christ alone, shall be the trembling sinner's stay.
Anon

THE PRESIDENT OF UGANDA

In 1998, President Y. K. Museveni, a Christian, described by Reuters news agency as 'one of the most outspoken proponents of change in Africa', gave a bold speech explaining how faith could transform the continent:

One of the most interesting facts about Jesus Christ is that in every nation on earth, no matter which religion is practised, he is regarded as the greatest authority on human relationships ever to have lived. His views on this subject transcend all cultures and religions and are accepted by all people. I'd like to pick up on three of his principles, which, if we can put them into practice, will help Africa. I'm speaking of forgiveness, humility and love.

Forgiveness: Jesus Christ is the only person who spoke of unconditional forgiveness, even towards personal enemies. How, in countries at war for generations, can any person or nation find peace unless we at some point forgive and leave God to judge over our enemies, if he so chooses. It has been discovered that, if we do not forgive, we hurt ourselves more than those we hate. I have reached the conclusion that Christ's message about forgiveness is the only practical solution for a nation's wounds, and the only way to true unity.

Humility: one of the greatest requirements for becoming a good leader. Many leaders follow their desire for power, their greed and their own interests. Once they achieve prominence, they suddenly forget the people around them, with their poverty and needs. They forget that they could become great instruments of help for their countries, and behave like small kings and dictators. Only if we humbly recognize that those with great responsibility are in truth only servants of God and people will we be able to lead our peoples out of their third-world existence into a new future. The Bible says: 'God withstands the proud and helps the humble.' If you have time to pray for me, please pray that God will give me the strength, wisdom and understanding to be humble.

Love: I find it fascinating to see that for centuries, those people who made great contributions to human development were united in their belief that life's highest goal is to seek God and to love him with all your heart, mind, soul and strength. I am thinking of Moses, Abraham, William Wilberforce and Mother Teresa. If we in our nations and societies would make a rule of loving God and one another, all problems would soon be solved.

Can we today decide to free Jesus Christ from the religious straitjacket into which we have forced him, and with him travel Africa's dusty roads, where he is much more at home?'

OLD TESTAMENT HEATHEN DEITIES

PEOPLE GROUP	CHIEF DEITY	OTHER DEITIES	SPHERE	RELATIONSHIP
Ammonite	Moloch			
Assyrians	Asshur			
Babylonians	Antu		Heaven	Husband/wife
	Eridu	Enlil	Earth	Husband/wife
	Marduk (Bel)	Damkina	Sun	Son/mother
	Sin	Ningal	Moon	Husband/wife
	Ishtar	Tammuz	Fertility	Husband/wife
	Allatu		Oceans	
	Nabu		Learning	
	Nusku		Fire	
Canaanites	El	Asherah	Creator	Husband/wife
		(Ashtoreth)		Offspring of
				El and Asherah
		Baal		
		Dagon		
		Resheph		
		Koshar		
		Mot		
Egyptians	Ra	Osiris	The dead	Sister/wife
		Horus	Fertility	Son of
				Ra/Osiris
		Anubis		
		Thoth		
		Maat	Truth	
		Nut	Sky	
		Shu	Air	
		Nu	Water	
		Geb	Earth	
		Apis		
		Mnevis		
Moabites	Chemosh			
Philistines	Dagon	Ashtoreth		
		Ekron		
		Baalzebu		

'GOD CHOSE THE WEAK THINGS OF THE WORLD TO SHAME THE STRONG…'

Many of the important figures in the Bible had a clear weakness:

Name	Weakness
Moses	Murderer
Timothy	Weak stomach
Paul	Thorn in the flesh
Jonah	Disobeyed God
David	Murderer and adulterer
Abraham	Too old to bear a son
Gideon	Scared
Amos	Peasant farmer
John Mark	Unreliable
Jacob	Liar
Jeremiah	Depressed and suicidal
Elijah	Burnt out
Noah	Drunkard
Saul	Consulted a witch
Hezekiah	Naive
James and John	Impulsive
Peter	Disloyal
Thomas	Doubter
Samson	Deceived
Ruth	Penniless widow

FROM THE MOUTHS OF BABES AND INFANTS

'In Sunday School they told us what you do. Who does it when you are on holiday?'

'I didn't think orange went with purple until I saw the sunset you made on Tuesday.'

'Are you really invisible or is that a trick?'

'Did you mean for the giraffe to look like that or was it an accident?'

'Who draws the lines around countries?'

'What does it mean, you are a jealous God? I thought you had everything.'

'Thank you for the baby brother, but what I prayed for was a puppy!'

'Dear God, please send me a pony. I never asked for anything before, you can look it up.'

'I bet it is very hard for you to love all of everybody in the whole world. There are only four people in our family and I can never do it.'

'Dear God, if you watch me in church on Sunday, I'll show you my new shoes.'

'We read at school that Thomas Edison made light. But in church they said you did it. So, I bet he stole your idea.'

BIBLE WEIGHTS AND MEASURES

UNIT	IMPERIAL	METRIC
Weight		
talent	75 pounds	34 kilograms
mina	1/2 pound	0.6 kilograms
hekel (2 bekahs)	2/5 ounce	11.5 grams
pim (2/3 shekel)	1/3 ounce	7.6 grams
bekah (10 gerahs)	1/5 ounce	5.5 grams
gerah	1/50 ounce	0.6 grams
Dry capacity		
cor (homer) (10 ephahs)	6 bushels	220 litres
lethek (5 ephahs)	3 bushels	110 litres
ephah (10 omers)	3/5 bushel	22 litres
seah (1/3 ephah)	7 quarts	7.3 litres
omer	2 quarts	2 litres
cab (1/18 ephah)	1 quart	1 litre
Liquid capacity		
bath (1 ephah)	6 gallons	22 litres
hin (1/6 bath)	4 quarts	4 litres
log (1/72 bath)	1/3 quart	0.3 litres
Length		
cubit	18 inches	0.5 metres
span	9 inches	23 centimetres
handbreadth	3 inches	8 centimetres

Note: This chart is based upon the best, most conservative information availabl

GOD IS…
Lord Almighty
   Omnipotent King
      Lion of Judah
         Rock of ages
           Prince of peace
             King of kings
               Lord of lords
                 Provider
                   Protector
                   Love
Reigning King of all the universe
   Father
      The First and Last
         The keeper of creation
           Unmoved
             Unchanged
               Undefeated
                 Never Undone
                 Light
                 Holy
Righteous
   Omniscient
      Eternal
         Guide
           Perfect
             Saviour
               Peace
               Joy
                 Redeemer
The Beginning and the End.
Anon

TEN TWENTIETH-CENTURY MARTYRS

On 9 July 1998, the Archbishop of Canterbury, in the presence of Queen Elizabeth II, unveiled statues of ten twentieth-century martyrs outside the west front of Westminster Abbey, London. The ten martyrs commemorated were:

Father Maximilian Kolbe (Zdunska Wola), a victim of Nazism in 1941. He offered his own life to save a fellow prisoner.

Manche Masemola, murdered by her parents for converting to Christianity in Transvaal (South Africa) in 1928.

Janani Luwum, a school teacher from Uganda, murdered in 1976 by the Idi Amin regime.

Grand Duchess Elizabeth of Russia, a victim of the Russian Revolution of 1918.

Dr Martin Luther King Jr, American preacher assassinated in Memphis in 1968.

Archbishop Oscar Romero of San Salvador, murdered in 1980.

Dietrich Bonhoeffer, German Pastor murdered by the Nazis in April 1945.

Esther John (Qamar Zia), Indian missionary, murdered in 1960.

Lucian Tapiedi, from Papua New Guinea, murdered by Japanese troops in 1942.

Wang Zhiming, Chinese pastor, executed by the authorities in 1973.

POPULAR BIBLE SAYINGS

IDIOM	REFERENCE
An eye for an eye	Exodus 21:24
A house divided against itself cannot stand	Matthew 12:25
Cast the first stone	John 8:7
Don't throw your pearls before swine	Matthew 7:6
He who fights with the sword will die by the sword	Matthew 26:52
It is more blessed to give than to receive	Acts 20:35
Labour of love	1 Thessalonians 1:3
Man does not live on bread alone	Deuteronomy 8:3; Matthew 4:4

No peace for the wicked	Isaiah 48:22
Pride comes before a fall	Proverbs 16:18
Red sky in the morning	Matthew 16:3
Salt of the earth	Matthew 5:13
Signs of the times	Matthew 16:3
Some fell on rocky ground	Matthew 13:5
Suffer fools gladly	2 Corinthians 11:19
The blind leading the blind	Matthew 15:14
There is nothing new under the sun	Ecclesiastes 1:9
The love of money is the root of all evil	1 Timothy 6:10
Thorn in the flesh	2 Corinthians 12:7

TYPOLOGY

The Gospels tell of Jesus' life on earth, but throughout the Bible, images (or types) of Christ exist to supplement our knowledge of him. A type is a representation of one thing by another, similar to an analogy. There are many 'types' of Christ throughout the scriptures – people, systems and institutions that were living prophecies of his life and teachings. Some examples of types of Christ are given below:

The serpent Moses lifted up in the desert to save the children of Israel is referred to by Jesus in John 3:14: 'Just as Moses lifted up the snake in the desert, so the Son of man must be lifted up.'

Jonah's sojourn inside a fish for three days and three nights predicts Jesus' three days and three nights in the heart of the earth.

Joseph the messianic patriarch was betrayed by his own (like Jesus), wrongly accused (like Jesus), humbled (like Jesus) and exalted (like Jesus).

The system of Old Testament offerings for sin, guilt, fellowship and peace prefigured the once-for-all sacrifice of the Son of man (Hebrews 9:11–14).

The Old Testament Law given by Moses prefigured the coming of Christ as the 'Living Word'.

JOB'S COMFORTERS

'You have heard of the endurance of Job, and you have seen the purpose of the Lord, how the Lord is compassionate and merciful' (James 5:11, NRSV).

Job was severely tested by God. He lost his family, possessions, health and status. His friends came to comfort him, but although they were good at analysing his downfall and pointing out his faults, they were not that good at empathizing with Job or suggesting solutions!

No thanks to his friends, Job survived his trials and maintained his faith in God: 'But he knows the way that I take; when he has tested me, I shall come out like gold' (Job 23:10, NRSV).

Eliphaz the Temanite 'comforts' Job in chapters 4 and 5.
Bildad the Shuhite 'comforts' Job in chapter 8.
Zophar the Naamathite 'comforts' Job in chapter 11.

'I have heard many things like these; miserable comforters are you all!' (Job 16:2)

THE CAMBRIDGE SEVEN

Recruited by Dr Schofield to serve God as members of the China Inland Mission in 1885, the Cambridge Seven were:

Charles Thomas Studd: brilliant England cricketer, sent home from China because of ill health. He went on to serve as a missionary to India and then to the Belgian Congo, where he died in 1931.

William Cassels: worked with Montague Beauchamp. Considered going to Africa as a missionary but opted for China.

Montague Beauchamp: worked with William Cassels. In 1900, he was evacuated because of uprisings against foreigners, but he went back to China in 1902. He returned to England in 1911 and served as a chaplain with the British Army.

Stanley P. Smith: went to North China. Became as fluent a preacher in Chinese as in English. Died in China on 31 January 1931.

Arthur Polhill-Turner: ordained as a minister in 1888 and moved to the densely populated countryside to reach as many people as he could with the gospel message. He died in 1935.

Cecil Polhill-Turner: brother of Arthur. Went to the China/Tibet border region. In 1900, his health failed and he was sent home to England and forbidden to return to China. But his heart was still in China and, throughout the rest of his life, he made seven prolonged missionary visits. He died in England in 1938.

Dixon Hoste: in 1903, he succeeded Hudson Taylor as Director of the China Inland Mission. For 30 years, he led the Mission, which made great advances, reaching many with the gospel before he retired in 1935. He died in London in May 1946.

THE PRODIGAL SON IN THE KEY OF F

Feeling footloose and frisky, a featherbrained fellow forced his fond father to fork over the farthings and flew far to foreign fields and frittered his fortune feasting fabulously with faithless friends.

Fleeced by his fellows in folly, and facing famine, he found himself a feed-flinger in a filthy farmyard. Fairly famishing, he fain would have filled his frame with foraged food from fodder fragments.

'Phooey, my father's flunkies fare far finer,' the frazzled fugitive forlornly fumbled, frankly facing facts. Frustrated by failure, and filled with foreboding, he fled forthwith to his family. Falling at his father's feet, he forlornly fumbled, 'Father, I've flunked, and fruitlessly forfeited family fellowship favour.'

The farsighted father, forestalling further flinching, frantically flagged the flunkies to fetch a fatling from the flock and fix a feast. The fugitive's faultfinding brother frowned on fickle forgiveness of former folderol.

But the faithful father figured, 'Filial fidelity is fine, but the fugitive is found! What forbids fervent festivity? Let flags be unfurled! Let fanfares flare!' Father's forgiveness formed the foundation for the former fugitive's future fortitude!
Timothy E. Fulop — adaptation of Luke 15:11–32

THE TWELVE TRIBES OF ISRAEL

The 12 sons of Jacob were the fathers of the 12 tribes of Israel, blessed by Jacob and, later, allocated areas of the Promised Land through the victories of Joshua. This is the order of the 12 tribes around the tabernacle (place of meeting):

Tribe	Mother	1st Numbering	2nd Numbering
Asher	Zilpah	41,500	53,400
Benjamin	Rachel	35,400	45,600
Dan	Bilhah	62,700	64,400
Gad	Zilpah	45,650	40,500
Joseph*	Rachel	–	–
Ephraim		40,500	32,500
Manasseh		52,700	46,800
Levi	Leah	Not numbered	Not numbered
Naphtali	Bilhah	53,400	45,400
Reuben	Leah	46,500	39,400
Simeon	Leah	59,300	22,200
Zebulun	Zilpah	57,400	60,500

*The sons of Joseph, Ephraim and Manasseh were each given a portion of land

CODEX

Def: **codex**:\Co'dex\ n. – an ancient manuscript of the sacred scriptures, or any part of them, particularly the New Testament.

Vaticanus	Dates from about the mid fourth century. Contains most of the Old Testament. Now in the Vatican.
Siniaticus	Discovered in 1844 in St Catherine's Monastery near Mount Sinai. Greek manuscript of the Old Testament.Contains the entire New Testament. Now in the British Museum(Codex 151).

Alexandricus, *Leningrad* or *Aleppo*	From the fifth Century. Once contained all New Testament, but some parts lost. Written in Cairo, probably, the oldest complete Hebrew bible still preserved. Considered one of the best examples of the Masoretic text. Now in St Petersburg, Russia, in the Russian National Library (Saltykov-Shchedrin), where it has been since the mid-1800s.
Argenteus (the 'Silver Bible')	Written in silver and gold letters on purple vellum. Thought to date from about 520. Contains most of the four Gospels. Located in Uppsala University Library (Sweden).

IMPORTANT BIBLE NUMBERS

One: Unity – one God, one body, one Spirit, one baptism, one faith.

Two: Accord – the disciples went in pairs; contrast – the Pharisee and the tax collector

Three: The number of power and emphasis: Father, Son and Holy Spirit. On the third day, Jesus rose from the dead; Saul (Paul) was blind for three days; Peter's vision was repeated three times; and a cord of three strands is not easily broken.

Four: The number of completion – four Gospels; four horsemen of the Apocalypse; Ezekiel's four living creatures.

Five: God's grace – David had five stones to slay Goliath; five loaves fed 5,000 men; five wise virgins brought spare oil for their lamps.

Six: The number of man. Adam was created on the sixth day; six stone jars were miraculously filled with wine in Cana; and there are six days for work.

Seven: The number of heavenly perfection. God blessed the seventh day and made it holy; Enoch was the seventh from Adam; Noah went into the ark with seven others; and only the Lamb of God (who has seven horns and seven eyes) can open the scroll with its seven seals.

Eight: A new start – a male child was circumcised on the eighth day; only eight people were saved in the ark.

Nine: God's blessing – nine fruits of the Spirit and nine gifts of the Spirit.

Ten: The number of order and judgment. There were ten Commandments; ten plagues upon Egypt; the faithful servant was made head of ten cities; and ten kings have ten horns in Revelation.

Twelve: God's divine purpose – 12 tribes of Israel, 12 disciples and twelve Judges. In Revelation, the Holy City has 12 foundations and 12 gates.

Forty: The number of testing – 40 days and nights of rain led to the Flood; Israel wandered for40 years; Jesus fasted for 40 days and nights before being tempted by the devil.

Fifty: Release – after 50 years, the land and slaves were liberated (the year of Jubilee).

Seventy: Judgment – there were 70 elders of Israel; the exiles returned to their land after 70 years; and Jesus appointed 70 to declare the kingdom of God in Babylon.

ST COLUMBA OF DONEGAL

These are the last words of St Columba, to his followers, before he died in AD 597:

Be at peace, and have unfeigned charity amongst yourselves, and if you follow the example of the Holy Fathers, God the Comforter of the good will be your helper, and I abiding with him will intercede for you, and he will not only give sufficient to supply the wants of the present life, but will also bestow on you the good and eternal rewards which are laid up for those who keep his commandments.

WELLS IN THE BIBLE

Then Israel sang this song:

'Spring up, O well!
Sing about it,

about the well that the princes dug,
that the nobles of the people sank —
the nobles with sceptres and staffs.'
Numbers 21:17–18

LOCATION	OCCASION	REFERENCE
Between Kadesh and Bered	God speaks to Hagar; the well is called Beer Lahai Roi (The Well of the Living One Who Sees Me)	Genesis 16:14
Beersheba	Abraham makes a covenant with Abimelech	Genesis 21:30–31
Nahor	Abraham's servant finds Rebekah	Genesis 24:20
Valley of Gerar	Isaac reopens his father's wells and worships the Lord	Genesis 26:18
Valley of Gerar	Isaac's servants dig a well	Genesis 26:32
Haran	Jacob meets Rachel	Genesis 29:9–10
Midian	Moses meets Zipporah	Exodus 2:15–21
Ramah (Secu)	Saul seeks David	1 Samuel 19:22
Sirah	Abner returns to meet Joab	2 Samuel 3:26
Bahurim	David's spies hide in the well	2 Samuel 17:18
Jerusalem	Jeremiah is trapped in the cistern	Jeremiah 38:6
Sychar	Jesus speaks to the woman at the well	John 4:4–26

THE TWELVE APOSTLES

NAME	ALSO CALLED	FROM	JOB	SYMBOL
Simon (heard)	Peter, Cephas (rock)	Bethsaida	Fisherman	Keys
Andrew (manly)		Bethsaida	Fisherman	Cross
James (Jacob)	Boanerges (sons of thunder)	Bethsaida	Fisherman	Staff
John (God is gracious)	Boanerges (sons of thunder)	Bethsaida —	Fisherman —	Chalice
James (Jacob)	Son of Alphaeus	—	—	Saw
Jude (praise)	Thaddeus, Lebbaeus	—	—	Carpenter's square
Philip (lover of horses)	—	Bethsaida	—	Two loaves
Bartholomew (son of Tolomei)	Nathanael	Cana, Galilee	—	Knife
Matthew (gift of God)	Levi	Capernaum	Tax collector	Money bags
Thomas (twin)	Didymus	Galilee	—	Spear
Simon (heard)	Zelotes	Galilee	—	Fish
Judas (praise)	Iscariot	Kerioth, Judea	—	Yellow shield
Matthias* (gift of God)	—	Jerusalem	—	Book and axe

* *Chosen to replace Judas Iscariot*

FAMOUS LAST WORDS

Thomas Becket: 'I commend myself to God.'

Anne Boleyn: 'Oh God, have pity on my soul. Oh God, have pity on my soul.'

Charles I: 'I die as a Christian.'

Robert the Bruce: 'Now, God be with you, my dear children.'

Giacomo Casanova: 'I have lived as a philosopher and die as a Christian.'

Thomas Cranmer: 'I see heaven open and Jesus on the right hand of God.'

Oliver Cromwell: 'My design is to make what haste I can to be gone.'

Dwight Eisenhower: 'I want to go. God, take me.'

Pope Gregory VII: 'I have loved justice and hated iniquity.'

Joan of Arc: 'Hold the cross high so I may see it through the flames!'

John Calvin: 'I am abundantly satisfied, since it is from thy hand.'

John Hus: 'O holy simplicity!'

John Knox: 'Live in Christ, live in Christ, and the flesh need not fear death.'

John Wesley: 'The best of all is, God is with us. Farewell! Farewell!'

Martin Luther: 'God is the Lord by whom we escape death.'

Charles Wesley: 'I am well satisfied with thy likeness – satisfied, satisfied.'

Voltaire (an atheist): 'I am abandoned by God and man.'

BIBLICAL INERRANCY

Def: **Inerrant**: \in'e'rrant\n.; – considered accurate, truthful, reliable, totally free of error, without mistake and absolutely authoritative.

1978 CHICAGO STATEMENT OF THE INTERNATIONAL COUNCIL ON BIBLICAL INERRANCY

1. God, who is Himself Truth and speaks truth only, has inspired Holy Scripture in order thereby to reveal Himself to lost mankind through Jesus Christ as Creator and Lord, Redeemer and Judge. Holy Scripture is God's witness to Himself.

2. Holy Scripture, being God's own Word, written by men prepared and superintended by His Spirit, is of infallible divine authority in all matters upon which it touches: It is to be believed, as God's instruction, in all that it affirms; obeyed, as God's command, in all that it requires; embraced, as God's pledge, in all that it promises.

3. The Holy Spirit, Scripture's divine Author, both authenticates it to us

by His inward witness and opens our minds to understand its meaning.

4. Being wholly and verbally God-given, Scripture is without error or fault in all its teaching, no less in what it states about God's acts in creation, about the events of world history, and about its own literary origins under God, than in its witness to God's saving grace in individual lives.

5. The authority of Scripture is inescapably impaired if this total divine inerrancy is in any way limited or disregarded, or made relative to a view of truth contrary to the Bible's own; and such lapses bring serious loss to both the individual and the Church.

PSALM 23: FRAE HEBREW INTIL SCOTTIS

I'm in the Maister's flock, He is my herd;
And sin' He loo'es His ain, I've a' that's best;
By caller burns He airts my thowless feet,
And in the guid green haughs, He bids me rest.
He kens my failin's, merks my ilka turn,
And whiles, when frae the track I gang astray,
Wi' tender care He taks me in His airms,
And sets me doon in His ain richteous way.
Though death suld cuist her shadow in my gate,
And eerie seem the valley, mirk and lang;
I'm suire nae hand daur fash or daunton me,
For Ye are there, my comfort and my sang
Ye've gien me meat amang my verra foes,
Ye've shoo'ered your blessin's on my worthless heid;
My cup o' joy is fu' and rinnin' owre,
My Maister's guidness, and His mercy strang,
Hae gane wi' me, and will through aa the days;
I've mair in Thee than meets my ilka need.
Till in His hame I dwall for evermair –
Mine then the bliss, but His be aa the praise!
William Landles

HEBRAIC BIBLE ORDER

SECTION	HEBREW	ENGLISH
TORAH – Law	Bereshith	Genesis
	Shemoth	Exodus
	Wayyiqra	Leviticus
	Bemidbar	Numbers
	Debarim	Deuteronomy
NEBIM – Former Prophets	Yehoshua	Joshua
	Shophetim	Judges
	Shemuel (1 and 2)	Samuel (1 and 2)
	Melakim (1 and 2)	Kings (1 and 2)
NEBIM – Latter Prophets	Yeshayahu	Isaiah
	Yirmeyahu	Jeremiah
	Yehezqel	Ezekiel
	Daniel*	Daniel
SHNEM ASAR – The Twelve	Hoshea	Hosea
	Joel	Joel
	Amos	Amos
	Obadyah	Obadiah
	Yonah	Jonah
	Mikah	Micah
	Nahum	Nahum
	Habaqquq	Habakkuk
	Tsephanyah	Zephaniah
	Haggai	Haggai
	Zekaryah	Zechariah
	Malaki	Malachi
KETHUBIM – Writings	Tehillim	Psalms
	Mishle	Proverbs
	Iyob	Job
	Shir haShirim	Song of Songs
	Ruth	Ruth
	Ekah	Lamentations
	Qoheleth	Ecclesiastes
	Esther	Esther
	Ezra-Nehemyah	Ezra-Nehemiah
	Dibre ha Yamim	Chronicles (1 and 2)

*Daniel is sometimes included in the Kethubim

SATANIC APPELLATIONS

Def: **Satan**\Sa'tan\ n.: Evil adversary of God and humanity, often identified with the leader of the fallen angels; the Devil.

Accuser	Revelation 12:10
Adversary	1 Job 1:6, 12
Angel of light	2 Corinthians 11:14-15
Abaddon	Revelation 9:11
Beelzebub	Matthew 12:24
Belial	2 Corinthians 6:15
Day Star	Isaiah 14:12
Devil	Hebrews 2:14
Diabolos	Revelation 12:9
Enemy	Matthew 13:39
Father of lies	John 8:44
God of this age	2 Corinthians 4:4
Ruler of the kingdom of the air	Ephesians 2:2
Prince of this world	John 12:31
Roaring lion	1 Peter 5:8
Satan	Zechariah 3:1
Spirit … at work in those who are disobedient	Ephesians 2:2
Tempter	1 Thessalonians 3:5

SEEING SALVATION

Stare at the four dots in the middle of the picture for about 30 seconds, then close your eyes. Keep them closed.

What do you see?

BIBLE FEATURES

Feature	Old Testament	New Testament	Total
Number of books	39	27	66
Chapters	929	270	1,199
Verses	23,214	7,931	31,145
Longest book	Psalms	Luke	
Middle book	Proverbs	2 Thessalonians	
Shortest book	Obadiah	3 John	
Middle chapter	Job 20	Romans 13 and 14	
Middle verse	1 Chronicles 26:17	Acts 11:17	
Longest verse	Esther 8:9	John 11:35	

AMAZING GRACE

John Newton, the son of a merchant-ship commander, composed the lyrics to this popular hymn around 1760 in Olney, England. The origin of the melody is unknown, but may be from an American folk song. The words are a testimony to Newton's life. On 10 May 1748, he nearly died off the coast of Sierra Leone while serving on a slave ship. The vessel went through a great storm and Newton summed up his experience with the line, 'Thro' many dangers, toils and snares, I have already come; 'tis grace has bro't me safe thus far, and grace will lead me home.'

A popular hymn at funerals, this is a list of ten celebrity funerals to have used 'Amazing Grace':

NAME	OCCUPATION	DATE
Stevie Ray Vaughan	Musician	1990
Albert King	Blues guitarist	1992
Alex Haley	Author	1992
Richard Nixon	President of the USA	1994
Bill Monroe	Bluegrass musician	1996
Sonny Bono	Singer	1998
Barry Goldwater	Senator	1998
Joe DiMaggio	Baseball player	1999
John Kennedy Jr	Publisher	1999
Pete Conrad	Astronaut	1999

AMERICAN BAPTIST RADIO WEATHER FORECAST

'And the New Year's Day weather… mostly cloudy with a 30 per cent chance of Jesus coming down on the clouds.'

CHRISTIAN CROWNS

Everlasting Crown – 1 Corinthians 9:25
Crown of rejoicing – 1 Thessalonians 2:19
Crown of righteousness – 2 Timothy 4:8
Crown of life – James 1:12
Crown of glory – 1 Peter 5:4

THE PORVOO CHURCHES

In 1992, official representatives of four Anglican Churches and eight Nordic and Baltic Churches produced a report on closer relations. The 'Porvoo Churches' (named after the town of Porvoo in Finland), have signed a Common Statement expressing their desire to 'move to visible communion'. The Porvoo Churches are:

CHURCH	DATE COMMON STATEMENT SIGNED
The Estonian Evangelical-Lutheran Church	19 April 1994
The Church of Sweden	24 August 1994
The Church of Norway	15 November 1994
The Scottish Episcopal Church	9 December 1994
The Church of Ireland	16 May 1995
The Anglican Church	9 July 1995
The Evangelical-Lutheran Church of Lithuania	29–30 July 1995
The Church in Wales	September 1995
The Evangelical-Lutheran Church of Iceland	17–27 October 1995
The Evangelical-Lutheran Church of Finland	8 November 1995

THE HERMIT OF LEBANON

Born in 1828, Joseph Makhlouf of Bkkakafra was the first confessor saint of the Lebanese Maronite Order of Monks. He became a novice monk at the age of 23 at the Monastery of Our Lady of Mayfouq, north of Jbeil, Lebanon. In 1853, he took vows of poverty, chastity and obedience, choosing the name of Charbel (after an old Oriental martyr). He was sent to the Monastery of Cyprian and Justina at Kfifan to finish his religious studies and was ordained a priest in 1859. For 23 years, his hermit life consisted of contemplation, manual work, fasting, continuous prayer, resting on a hard couch and wearing a hair shirt.

Miracles attributed to Joseph Makhlouf (Father Charbel) include:

❏ Curing a mad person by prayer.

❏ Commanding a snake to stop attacking his brethren.

❏ Clearing a field of grasshoppers by using holy water.

❏ Lighting his lamp with water.

❏ Knowing that a sick person had died before entering their house.

After his death in 1898, his followers reported hundreds of miracles, including:

❏ An extraordinary brightness surrounding his tomb.

❏ A blood-like liquid dripping from his body four months after his death. This liquid was taken devoutly in a cloth, which often gave relief to the sick and sometimes cured them.

❏ Sister Maria Abel Kamari, who was lame, was cured after visiting the saint's tomb in 1950.

❏ Alessandro O'Beid, a blind man, received his sight after visiting the saint's tomb in 1950.

Joseph was beatified by Pope Paul VI on 5 December 1965. In his address, His Holiness paid this tribute to the holy hermit of Lebanon:

> 'May St Charbel draw us after him along the path of sanctity, where silent prayer in the presence of God has its own particular place. May he make us understand, in a world largely fascinated by wealth and comfort, the paramount value of poverty, penance and asceticism, to liberate the soul in its ascent to God. The practice of these virtues is indeed different according to the various states of life and responsibilities of people. But no Christian can ignore them if he wants to follow Our Lord.'

SIMON THE STYLITE

Born in AD 392, Simon is the most famous of the stylites, or saints who spent their days seated on high platforms or pillars. At the age of 13, Simon gave himself over to the service of God in the Syrian desert. When he later sought solitude away from the crowds that pressed around him, he established himself on a pillar which grew higher and higher above the crowds until it reached 60 feet. He thus lived between heaven and earth for about forty years, preaching and exhorting the crowds from high upon his pillar. Numerous individuals who came to him were converted by his preaching. He died in AD 459.

WELSH SAINTS THROUGH THE YEAR

Date	Saint	Period
19 January	Branwaladr	Sixth-century monk, bishop of Jersey
29 January	Gildas the Wise	Died in 570. Shrine is at St Gildas de Rhuys
1 February	Seirol	Sixth-century – abbot of Penmon
17 February	Curig	Sixth-century Irish missionary to Wales
1 March	Dewi	Sixth-century abbot – patron saint of Wales
2 March	Non	Mother of Dewi
9 April	Madrun	Fifth-century nun
21 April	Beuno	Seventh-century abbot
21 May	Collen	Sixth-century hermit
29 May	Buryan	Fifth-century convert of Patrick
4 June	Petroc	Seventh-century martyr
28 June	Austell	Sixth-century disciple of Samson
8 July	Urith	Eighth-century martyr
28 July	Samson	Sixth-century Bishop of Dol (Brittany)
1 August	Eiluned	Sixth-century virgin and martyr
23 August	Tydfil	Sixth-century virgin and martyr
12 September	Elvis	Seventh-century bishop
25 September	Cadoc	Sixth-century abbot, author of *Cattwg Doeth*
14 October	Selyf	Sixth-century king of Cornwall
18 October	Gwen	Wife of Selyf
1 November	Cadfan	Sixth-century abbot from Twyn
15 November	Malo	Sixth-century apostle of Brittany
5 December	Justinian	Sixth-century hermit
9 December	Buddoc	Sixth-century bishop of Dol (Brittany)

WORLD WATCH LIST

The Christian charity Open Doors International issues a World Watch List every year to highlight 50 areas of the world where Christians face severe persecution. The list is compiled from a specially designed 49-point questionnaire that assesses the official status of Christians, their daily privations, the role of the church in society, the availability of Christian literature and freedom of assembly.

The table below from January 2004 lists the top 20 countries where Christians experience the severest persecution.

RANK	COUNTRY	RELIGION/REGIME
1	North Korea	Communist
2	Saudi Arabia	Islam
3	Laos	Communist
4	Vietnam (Highlands)	Communist
5	Iran	Islam
6	Turkmenistan	Islam
7	Maldives	Islam
8	Bhutan	Buddhist
9	Myanmar (Burma)	Islam
10	China	Communist
11	Somalia	Islam
12	Pakistan	Islam
13	Afghanistan	Islam
14	Comoros	Islam
15	Sudan	Islam
16	Uzbekistan	Communist
17	Yemen	Islam
18	Eritrea	Islam
19	Egypt	Islam
20	Azerbaijan	Communist

PLACES TO VISIT

PLACE	DETAILS/REASON
Israel	To see where some of the events of the Bible took place.
Rome, Italy	Home of the pope and where St Peter was martyred.
Lourdes, France	A place of miraculous healings since Bernadette Soubirous had a vision of Jesus' mother in 1858.
Santiago de Compostela, Spain	Where the apostle James was buried.
Canterbury, England	Where Archbishop Thomas à Becket was martyred.
Walsingham, England	To see the shrines inspired by Richeldis de Faverches' vision of Jesus' mother in 1061.
Iona, Scotland	To see St Columba's monastery from 530.
Knock, Eire	In 1879, a group of young people witnessed a holy vision here.
St David's, Wales	The home of the patron saint of Wales.
Fatima, Portugal	Three shepherd children, Lucia, Jacinta and Francisco, received visions of the Virgin Mary here, in October 1917.
Guadalupe, Mexico	In December 1531, the Virgin Mary appeared to Juan Diego here.
Croatia, Medjugorje	The Virgin Mary appeared to six youngsters here on 24 June 1981.
Oberammagau, Austria	To see the passion play inspired by the village's miraculous deliverance from the Plague in 1633.

CHURCH COUNCILS

The first church council was held in Jerusalem to decide the conditions for gentiles (non-Jewish people) to enter the church (Acts 15). Other notable councils include:

DATE	EVENT	OUTCOME
325	Council of Nicea	Nicene Creed agreed
364	Council of Laodicea	Sunday adopted as Sabbath day
381	First Council of Constantinople	Nicene Creed confirmed
394	Council of Carthage	The Catholic doctrine of purgatory adopted
431	Council of Ephesus	Nestorianism denied
451	Council of Chalcedon	Ruled on the divinity and humanity of Christ
553	Second Council of Constantinople	To settle disputes between Western (Roman Catholic) and Eastern (Orthodox) wings of Christianity
680	Third Council of Constantinople	Dealt with Monotheletism
787	Second Council of Nicea	Last of seven councils recognized by both Roman Catholic and Orthodox denominations
869	Fourth Council of Constantinople	Restoration of St Ignatius
1085	Council of Clermont	The First Crusade launched
1123	First Lateran Council	Concordat of Worms confirmed
1139	Second Lateran Council	To bridge the gulf between Catholic and Orthodox denominations
1170	Third Lateran Council	Established rules for electing the pope
1215	Fourth Lateran Council	Recognized the necessity of the eucharist
1408	Council of Oxford	Prohibited translation of the scriptures into common language
1417	Council of Constance	Tried and condemned John Hus
1545	Council of Trent	Defined official Roman Catholic theology
1869	First Vatican Council	Discussed ecumenicalism
1962	Second Vatican Council	Produced 16 documents designed to revitalize the church

TEN END-TIME PROPHECIES

The Bible has much to say about future events. Over time, many people have tried to interpret how and when the end of this present age will come, with widely differing conclusions. Here are ten examples of what the Bible says the future holds:

1. Jerusalem will be besieged by surrounding nations (Zechariah 12:1–5).

2. Israel will face a 200 million strong army (Revelation 9:16).

3. The river Euphrates will dry up allowing the invaders to attack Israel (Revelation 16:12).

4. The nations that attacked Jerusalem will be punished (Zechariah 14:12).

5. The nation of Israel will be miraculously delivered and revived (Luke 21:29-31).

6. The whole planet will be affected (Revelation 11:9–10).

7. Global preaching of the Gospel (Matthew 24:14).

8. People will be forced to have a mark on their forehead or hand (Revelation 13:16–18).

9. The nations of the world will go to Israel for blessing (Zechariah 8:22).

10. The promised Messiah will return to Israel (Jeremiah 23:3–6).

PRECISE DATING

James Ussher (1581–1656), archbishop of Armagh in Ireland, calculated that the creation of the world took place on Sunday 23 October in the year 4004 BC.

T. S. ELIOT

Nobel Laureate American-born Thomas Stearns Eliot (1888–1965) described himself as Anglo-Catholic. He was confirmed in the Anglican Church in 1927, the same year that he adopted British citizenship.

One of the most influential writers of the last century, Eliot is best known for:

'The Love Song of J. Alfred Prufrock' – 1915

'The Waste Land' – 1922

Murder in The Cathedral – 1935

Old Possum's Book of Practical Cats – 1939

The Four Quartets – 1943

Extract from 'The Journey of the Magi' (1927):

> Birth or Death? There was a Birth, certainly.
> We had evidence and no doubt. I had seen birth and death
> But had thought they were different; this Birth was
> Hard and bitter agony for us, like Death, our death.
> We returned to our places, these Kingdoms,
> But no longer at ease here, in the old dispensation,
> With an alien people clutching their gods.
> I should be glad of another death.

MUSICAL INSTRUMENTS

Music has always been an important aspect of faith. Jubal is recognized in Genesis as the father of 'all who play the pipe and lyre'. There are many examples of musical instruments in biblical times, including:

Dulcimer: bagpipes.

Halil: a woodwind pipe with holes that produced sound from a reed.

Hazora: a bronze or silver trumpet used in battle.

Kinnor: a harp-like instrument held in the crook of one arm and played with the other hand or plucked with a plectrum-like accessory. Some models took the shape of the Sea of Galilee, hence the appellation *Kinneret.*

Menaanim: a metal, drum-like percussion instrument.

Nevel: a 12-stringed harp–lyre combination, shaped like a wineskin.

Paamonim: bells attached to priestly robes.

Queren: a wind instrument used in worship, made from animal horn. Known as a shophar if the horn was from a ram.

Systrum: a sliding rattle.

Tziltzilim: copper cymbals used to mark the start and end of sung psalms.

Tof: similar to a timbrel or tambourine.

CLASSIFICATION OF RELICS

Def. **Relic** \Rel'ic\n.; – an object of religious veneration, especially a piece of the body or a personal item of a saint.

The Roman Catholic Church has, over the centuries, developed the following classification system for holy relics. It is forbidden for first and second-class relics to be sold. In the Middle Ages, the most sought-after relic was a piece of the cross of Christ.

First-class relics	Actual part of a saint, such as limb, hair or bone; for example, the Holy Prepuce (or Holy Foreskin) of Jesus
Second-class relics	Any item worn by a saint
Third-class relics	First division: a piece of cloth in contact with the body of a saint, for example the Shroud of Turin, believed by some to be the burial cloth of Christ
	Second division: a piece of cloth brought to the shrine (or site of the vision) of the saint

THE PEOPLE'S PRIEST

Ulrich Zwingli (1484–1531), a contemporary of Martin Luther, was appointed the people's priest at the Great Minster Church in Zürich in 1519. His sermons from that pulpit extended the Lutheran Reformation throughout Switzerland. He urged his congregation to understand the Bible for themselves, called for a return to the principles of the New Testament and taught the Lord's supper as a memorial.

Like Luther, he attacked the practice of Catholic-approved indulgences. In 1522, he protested against the Catholic practice of fasting at Lent, arguing that it is not commanded in the New Testament. His opposition to the established church led to Zürich becoming the first Protestant state, effectively a theocracy, outside Germany in 1523.

He disagreed with Luther over the eucharist. Luther believed in the Catholic doctrine of transubstantiation, that the bread and wine were actually changed into the body and blood of Christ. Zwingli maintained that the eucharist simply *symbolized* the sacrifice of Christ. Both men met at Marburg to attempt reconciliation in 1529. However, this did not lead to agreement, and their differences led to an early split in the Protestant movement.

Zwingli continued with his preaching and succeeded in persuading six out of the 13 Swiss localities or cantons to break away from Catholic rule. The remaining cantons, known as the Forest Cantons, remained staunchly Catholic. The ensuing tension led to civil war. Zwingli was wounded at Kappel em Albis in 1531 and later killed by the victorious Forest Canton forces. Today, Switzerland remains split along Protestant and Catholic lines.

THE GOLDEN LEGEND

In 1260, Jacobus de Voragine (Archbishop of Genoa, 1292–8) wrote the most famous work about the lives of the saints, called *Legenda Sanctorum* or *Legenda Aurea – The Golden Legend,* because readers considered its contents worth their weight in gold. This work was the most printed book in Europe in the Middle Ages and one of the first to be produced by William Caxton.

The Golden Legend consists of 177 chapters and details of the lives of many holy men and women, including:

Paul the first hermit

The translation of St Remigius

The chairing of St Peter

The seven Maccabees

The intervention of St Stephen, Protomartyr

The four crowned martyrs

The Venerable Bede

Antony of Egypt

The decollation of St John the Baptist

The translation of St Thomas of Canterbury

John the Almoner

The conversion of Paul

CHURCH FATHERS

After the deaths of the apostles, holy men gave theological and pastoral guidance that helped establish the early church. These men, later known as the Church Fathers, wrote to correct errors, enforce order and encourage their brethren. They include:

Ignatius of Antioch

Irenaeus of Lyons

Athanasius of Alexandria

Basil the Great

Gregory of Nyssa

Gregory the Theologian

John Chrysostom

Cyril of Alexandria

Cyril of Jerusalem

Maximus the Confessor

John of Damascus

Photius of Constantinople

Gregory Palamas

Antony of Egypt

Macarius of Egypt

John of the Ladder

Isaac of Syria

Ephraim of Syria

Simeon the New Theologian

THE PRAYER OF JABEZ

In 2001, American Bruce Wilkinson published a book called *The Prayer of Jabez: Breaking Through to the Blessed Life*, based on a little-known Bible verse about an obscure person mentioned only twice in the Bible. *The Prayer of Jabez* book sold over 13 million copies, and led to *The Prayer of Jabez Bible Study*, *The Prayer of Jabez for Women* (by Wilkinson's wife), a 90-minute audio cassette, a video and a musical companion, *The Prayer of Jabez Music*.

Jabez cried out to the God of Israel, 'Oh, that you would bless me and enlarge my territory! Let your hand be with me, and keep me from harm so that I will be free from pain.' And God granted his request.
1 Chronicles 4:10

FAVOURITE HYMNS

Here are Britain's 20 favourite hymns, as voted by viewers of the BBC's *Songs of Praise* programme:

O Lord My God, when I in awesome wonder

Dear Lord and Father of Mankind

The day thou gavest, Lord, is ended

Great is thy faithfulness, O God my Father

Be still, for the presence of the Lord

What a friend we have in Jesus

Make me a channel of your peace

Love divine, all loves excelling

O love that wilt not let me go

On a hill far away stood an old rugged cross

Guide me, O thou great Redeemer

And can it be that I should gain

All things bright and beautiful

Abide with me; fast falls the eventide

And did those feet in ancient time (Jerusalem)

Be thou my vision, O Lord of my heart

I, the Lord of sea and sky (Here I am, Lord)

Lord, for the years

When I survey the wondrous cross

Lord, the light of your love is shining (Shine, Jesus, shine)

SOME PLANTS OF THE BIBLE

Popular Name	Botanical Name
Aloe	*Aquilaria agallocha*
Arbor-vitæ	*Thuja articulate*
Barley	*Hordeum*
Bearded darnel	*Lolium temulentum*
Blackberry	*Rubus*
Carob	*Ceratonia siliqua*
Cumin	*Cuminum cyminum*
Dill	*Anethum graveolens*
Fig	*Ficus carica*

Land-caltrop	*Tribulus terrestris*
Lily	*Lilium candidum*
Manna	*Tamarix mannifera*
Mint	*Mentha*
Mulberry	*Morus nigra*
Mustard	*Sinapis*
Palm	*Phœnix dactylifera*
Reed	*Arundo donax*
Rue	*Ruta*
Spikenard	*Nardostachys jatamansi*
Sycamore	*Ficus sycomorus*
Wheat, grain	*Triticum*
Wild marjoram	*Origanum maru*
Wild olive	*Olea europæ*
Wormwood	*Artemisia*

CLEAN AND UNCLEAN ANIMALS

Animals in the Bible were classified clean or unclean for hygiene, dietary and symbolic purposes. The distinction between clean and unclean is made first in Genesis 7:2–3, when Noah is commanded to take seven pairs of all clean animals and two pairs of all unclean animals. From this point, the principle of distinguishing between unclean and clean animals is established and further detailed in the Law.

ANIMAL CATEGORY	CLEAN	UNCLEAN
Quadrupeds	Those that chew the cud and divide the hoof, for example sheep, ox, wild goat and antelope	Camel, coney, hare and swine

ANIMAL CATEGORY	CLEAN	UNCLEAN
Fish	Whatever has fins and scales, and lives in the seas and rivers	Anything that does not have fins and scales
Birds	Any bird that is not a bird of prey; for example, poultry and pigeon	All birds of prey
Creeping things	Any animal that goes upon all fours with stomach off the ground, for example the locust	Anything that crawls, for example lizard, weasel, mouse and chameleon

EVENTS IN JESUS' FINAL WEEK

The three and a half years of Jesus' earthly ministry culminated in the most amazing events ever witnessed. The days leading up to the crucifixion and resurrection of Jesus were packed with drama, teaching, betrayal, zeal, anguish and triumph. Here is a summary of that fateful week:

Sunday	Triumphal entry into Jerusalem (Matthew 21:1–11)
Monday	Clearing the Temple (Mark 11:12–19)
Tuesday	Teaching at the Mount of Olives (Matthew 24:1–35)
Thursday	The last supper (Matthew 26:17–30)
	Betrayal and arrest (Mark 14:43–72)
Friday	Trials (John 18:28;19:16)
	Crucifixion (Matthew 27:32–56)
Sunday	Resurrection and appearances to the disciples (Luke 24:1–43)

ABBÉ GEORGES LE MAITRE

Probably the most famous Belgian of the twentieth century, Le Maitre (1894–1966) was a man of remarkable talents:

He was ordained as a Catholic priest in 1922.

He became Professor of Astrophysics at the University of Louvain (Belgium) in 1927.

He originated the theory of the expanding universe ('The Big Bang')which clarified Einstein's theory of relativity.

He travelled with Einstein across America in 1933 to explain his theories. After one seminar in California, Einstein applauded the Belgian, commenting that the expanding universe theory was, '... the most beautiful and satisfactory explanation of creation to which I have ever listened.'

In 1934, he was awarded the Gregor Mendal Medal in recognition of his scientific achievements and religious convictions.

WORDS OF WISDOM

LUDWIG VAN BEETHOVEN
No friend have I. I must live by myself alone; but I know well that God is nearer to me than others in my art, so I will walk fearlessly with him. I have always known and understood him.

AGATHA CHRISTIE
If you love, you will suffer, and if you do not love, you do not know the meaning of a Christian life.

CHARLES DICKENS
The New Testament is the very best book that ever was or ever will be known in the world.

WOLFGANG AMADEUS MOZART
It is a great consolation for me to remember that the Lord, to whom I had drawn near in humble and childlike faith, has suffered and died for me, and that he will look on me in love and compassion.

MARK TWAIN
If the ten commandments were not written by Moses, then they were written by another fellow of the same name.

GARTH BROOKS
Some of God's greatest gifts are unanswered prayers.

BLAISE PASCAL
Jesus Christ is the centre of everything, and the object of everything, and he that does not know him knows nothing of nature and nothing of himself.

BASQUE PROVERB
God is a good worker – but he loves to be helped.

PASTOR MARTIN NIEMÖLLER
In Germany they came first for the Communists and I didn't speak up because I wasn't a Communist. Then they came for the Jews and I didn't speak up because I wasn't a Jew. Then they came for the trade unionists and I didn't speak up because I wasn't a trade unionist. Then they came for the Catholics and I didn't speak up because I was a Protestant. Then they came for me – and by that time no one was left to speak up.

SIR THOMAS MORE
We cannot go to heaven on feather beds.

CARDINAL NEWMAN
There are no short roads to heaven, but there are sure ones.

WOODY ALLEN QUOTES

Not only is there no God, but try getting a plumber on weekends.
Getting Even, 1971

If only God would give me some clear sign! Like making a large deposit in my name at a Swiss bank.
New Yorker, 1973

How can I believe in God when just last week I got my tongue
caught in the roller of an electric typewriter?
Without Feathers, 1975

The chief problem about death, incidentally, is the fear that
there may be no afterlife – a depressing thought, particularly for
those who have bothered to shave. Also, there is the fear that
there is an afterlife but no one will know where it's being held.
Without Feathers, 1975

As the poet said, 'Only God can make a tree', probably because
it's so hard to figure out how to get the bark on.
Source unknown

To you I'm an atheist; to God, I'm the Loyal Opposition.
Source unknown

I don't want to achieve immortality through my work... I want
to achieve it through not dying.
The Columbia Dictionary of Quotations, 1975

The lion and the calf will lie down together – but the calf won't
get much sleep.
Without Feathers, 1975

CHRISTIAN PIONEERS

❑ Gladys Aylward (1902–70) – missionary to China

❑ Wellesley Bailey (1846–1937) – founder of the Leprosy Mission

❑ Agnes Gonxha Bojaxhiu (Mother Teresa) (1910–97) –
missionary to India

❑ David Brainerd (1718–47) – missionary to American Indians

❑ Jim Elliot (1927–56) – missionary to Ecuador

❑ Christmas Evans (1766–1838) – Welsh Baptist preacher

❑ Eva French (1869–1960) – missionary to China

❑ Elizabeth Fry (1780–1845) – prison reformer

❏ James Gilmour (1843–91) – missionary to Mongolia

❏ Adoniram Judson (1788–1850) – missionary to Burma

❏ Ann Judson (1789–1826) – missionary to India

❏ John Knox (1513–72) – Scottish reformer

❏ Eric Liddell (1902–45) – Olympian and missionary to China

❏ David Livingstone (1813–73) – missionary to Africa

❏ George Müller (1805–98) – founder of care homes for orphans

❏ Florence Nightingale (1820–1910) – nurse in Balaclava

❏ Mary Slessor (1848–1915) – missionary to Africa

❏ Hudson Taylor (1832–1905) – missionary to China

❏ Lillian Trasher (1887–1961) – missionary to Egypt

❏ George Whitefield (1714–70) – revival preacher

❏ Smith Wigglesworth (1859–1947) – evangelist and miracle worker

THEOPHANIES

Theophany refers to the appearance of Jesus Christ in the Old Testament. John 1:18 declares that 'No one has ever seen God, but God the One and Only, who is at the Father's side, has made him known.' Yet the Old Testament contains many appearances of the Lord God and the angel of the Lord. Since this cannot be God the Father, theologians recognize these appearances as the preincarnate Lord Jesus. Notable theophanies occur as follows:

PROMISE OF A SON

Then the Lord said, 'I will surely return to you about this time next year, and Sarah your wife will have a son.'
Genesis 18:10

ENCOURAGEMENT FOR JACOB

Then the man said, 'Your name will no longer be Jacob, but Israel, because you have struggled with God and with men and have overcome.'
Genesis 32:28

THE PROMISE OF A DELIVERER FOR ISRAEL

Then Manoah took a young goat, together with the grain offering, and sacrificed it on a rock to the Lord. And the Lord did an amazing thing while Manoah and his wife watched: as the flame blazed up from the altar towards heaven, the angel of the Lord ascended in the flame. Seeing this, Manoah and his wife fell with their faces to the ground. When the angel of the Lord did not show himself again to Manoah and his wife, Manoah realized that it was the angel of the Lord. 'We are doomed to die!' he said to his wife. 'We have seen God!'

Judges 13:19–22

DEFENDING THE PEOPLE OF GOD

Then the Lord opened Balaam's eyes, and he saw the angel of the Lord standing in the road with his sword drawn. So he bowed low and fell face down.

Numbers 22:31

ENCOURAGEMENT TO RISE UP AGAINST THE MIDIANITES

When the angel of the Lord appeared to Gideon, he said, 'The Lord is with you, mighty warrior.'

Judges 6:12

CHRISTIANS IN SCIENCE

Christians in Science is an organization of over 600 scientists, philosophers, theologians and others who have an interest in the interface between science and Christian faith. A journal called *Science and Christian Belief* is produced twice a year covering articles such as:

❏ A Still-Bent World: Some Reflections on Current Environmental Issues

❏ A Theological Perspective on Barrow and Tipler's: The Anthropic Cosmological Principle

❏ Capra on Eastern Mysticism and Modern Physics: A Critique

❏ What Happens When We Pray?

❏ Creatio Continua and Divine Action

❏ The Search for Extraterrestrial Intelligence and the Christian Doctrine of Redemption

POPULAR CHRISTIAN WEDDING MUSIC

THE PRELUDE
'Canon in D' by Pachelbel
'Holsworthy Church Bells' by Wesley
'Nimrod' from *Enigma Variations* by Elgar
'Greensleeves' by Williams
'Sheep May Safely Graze' by Bach

THE PROCESSIONAL
'Wedding March' from *Lohengrin* by Wagner
'Arrival of the Queen of Sheba' by Handel
'Trumpet Voluntary' by Stanley
'I Was Glad' by Parry
'Hornpipe' from the *Water Music* by Handel

THE SIGNING OF THE REGISTER
'Sheep May Safely Graze' by Bach
'Jesu Joy of Man's Desiring' by Bach
'Exultate Jubilate' by Mozart
'The Lord Bless You and Keep You' by Rutter
'Ave Verum Corpus' by Mozart

THE RECESSIONAL
'Grand March' from *Le Prophete* by Meyerbeer
'Fanfare' by Whitlock
'The Choral Symphony' by Beethoven
'March from Scipio' by Handel
'Hallelujah Chorus' from *Messiah* by Handel

MARTIN LUTHER KING JR

Michael King was born in 1929 in Atlanta, Georgia, into a family of Baptist clergy. In 1935, his father changed that name to Martin Luther, after the great German reformer.

A gifted student, King gained his doctorate from Boston University and became pastor of Dexter Avenue Baptist Church in Montgomery, Alabama, in 1954. Through his championing of civil rights, Martin Luther King became the leader of the most significant social justice movement of the twentieth century. It came about in this way.

In 1955, Mrs Rosa Parks, a black woman, sat at the front of a public bus. At that time, because of racial segregation, only white people were allowed to sit at the front. Black people had to sit at the back. Mrs Parks's arrest led to a black boycott of the Montgomery bus system. As a local pastor, Martin Luther King supported Mrs Parks. After a year-long boycott, the authorities relented and King was thrust, inadvertently, into the forefront of the growing civil rights movement.

Martin Luther King was a follower of the passive resistance methods of Ghandi. He travelled throughout America with a message of peaceful resistance, inspiring supporters to overcome evil with good. Not everyone was won over and, in 1958, King was stabbed in the chest.

In April 1963, King was imprisoned for participating in an anti segregation protest. Following his release, over 3,000 supporters marched and prayed for justice and freedom. Faced with this level of protest, the authorities relented and lifted segregation barriers in schools, restaurants, shops and workplaces. King had shown that the way of peace could work, despite overwhelming odds.

The civil rights movement arranged a celebration march in Washington on 28 August 1963. Over 250,000 people attended and heard King deliver one of the most memorable speeches of the twentieth century. Abandoning his notes, King shared his dream of a society united by the Christian message.

The march and speech led to the Civil Rights Act in 1964, banning segregation in many areas of life. However, King still had objectors and, on 4 April 1968, he was assassinated by James Earl Ray.

Over 100,000 people attended his funeral and today his peaceful legacy is continued by many organizations such as The King Center in

Atlanta. Since 1986, the third Monday of January is an American national holiday to commemorate the life and work of Martin Luther King Jr.

FAITH AND WORKS

By faith we must serve Him,
Who served us so well;
Who by dying and rising
Has saved us from Hell;
But ne'er let flesh be the fire
To gain His reward;
Nor trust human attainment,
And risk the Law's sword.
Wear His yoke willingly
And in love obey
Be filled with His Spirit
And walk in his Way.
David Chapman

FAMOUS EPITAPHS

Good friend for Jesus' sake forbear
To dig the dust enclosed here.
Blest be the man that spares these stones
And cursed be he that moves my bones.
William Shakespeare

Man must endure his going hence.
C. S. Lewis

God said, 'Let Newton be!' and all was light.
written by Alexander Pope of Sir Isaac Newton

Here lies the body of Jonathan Swift, Professor of Holy Theology, for thirty years Dean of this cathedral church, where savage indignation can tear his heart no more. Go, traveller, and if you can, imitate one who with his utmost strength protected liberty.
Jonathan Swift

I am ready to meet my Maker. Whether my Maker is prepared for the great ordeal of meeting me is another matter.
Winston Churchill

Lector, si monumentum requiris circumspice

(Reader, if you seek his monument look around you. Interred in St. Paul's Cathedral of which he was the architect)
Sir Christopher Wren

If I should die, think only this of me:
That there's some corner of a foreign field
That is for ever England.
Rupert Brooke

MORE CHURCH BULLETIN FUNNIES

The concert held in Fellowship Hall was a great success. Special thanks are due to the minister's daughter, who laboured the whole evening at the piano, which as usual fell upon her.

22 members were present at the church meeting held at the home of Mrs Marsha Crutchfield last evening. Mrs Crutchfield and Mrs Rankin sang a duet, The Lord Knows Why.

The juniors will be presenting Shakespeare's *Hamlet* in the church basement on Friday at 7 p.m. The congregation is invited to attend this tragedy.

Scouts are saving aluminium cans, bottles and other items to be recycled. Proceeds will be used to cripple children.

The third verse of Blessed Assurance will be sung without musical accomplishment.

The outreach committee has enlisted 25 visitors to make calls on people who are not afflicted with any church.

This afternoon there will be a meeting in the South and North ends of the church. Children will be baptized at both ends.

One day a lady criticized D.L. Moody, the great American evangelist, for his methods of winning people to the Lord.

Moody's reply was 'I agree with you. I don't like the way I do it either. Tell me, how do you do it?'

The lady replied, 'I don't do it.'

Moody responded, 'I like my way of doing it better than your way of not doing it.'

OCCUPATIONAL HYMNS

DENTISTS: Crown Him With Many Crowns

WEATHER FORECASTERS: There Shall Be Showers of Blessing

BUILDERS: The Church's One Foundation

TAILORS: Holy, Holy, Holy

GOLFERS: There is a Green Hill Far Away

POLITICIANS: Standing on the Promises

OPTICIANS: Open My Eyes That I Might See

TAX COLLECTORS: I Surrender All

GOSSIPS: Pass it on

ELECTRICIANS: Send the Light

LIBRARIANS: Whispering Hope

PILOTS: Closer My God To Thee

DOCTORS: Revive Us Again

JUDGES: Almost Persuaded

ARCHITECTS: How Firm a Foundation

POSTAL WORKERS: So Send I You

WAITERS: Fill My Cup, Lord

LIFEGUARDS: Rescue the Perishing

CRIMINALS: Search Me, O God

COBBLERS: It is Well with My Soul

TRAVEL AGENT: Anywhere with Jesus

GEOLOGISTS: Rock of Ages

LINGUISTS: O for a Thousand Tongues

NOAH'S EXCUSES FOR NOT COMPLETING THE ARK ON TIME

And the Lord said unto Noah: 'Where is the ark which I have commanded thee to build?'

And Noah said unto the Lord, 'Verily, I have had three carpenters off ill. The gopherwood supplier hath let me down – yea, even though the gopherwood hath been on order for nigh upon 50 years. What can I do O Lord?'

And God said unto Noah: 'I want that ark finished even after seven days and seven nights.'

And Noah said: 'It will be so.' And it was not so.

And the Lord said unto Noah: 'What seemeth to be the trouble this time?'

And Noah said unto the Lord: 'Mine subcontractor hath gone bankrupt. The pitch which Thou commandest me to put on the outside of the ark hath not arrived. The plumber hath gone on strike. Shem, my son who helpeth me on the ark side of the business, hath formed a pop group with his brothers Ham and Japheth. Lord, I am undone.'

And the Lord grew angry and said: 'And what about the animals, the male and female of every sort that I ordered to come unto thee to keep their seed upon the face of the earth?'

And Noah said: 'They have been delivered unto the wrong address but should arriveth on Friday.'

And the Lord said: 'How about the unicorns, and the fowls of the air by seven?'

And Noah wrung his hands and wept, saying: 'Lord, unicorns are a discontinued line, thou canst not get them for love nor money. And fowls of the air are sold only in half-dozens. Lord, Lord, Thou knowest how it is.'

And the Lord in his wisdom said: 'Noah, my son, I knowest, Why else dost thou think I have caused a flood to descend upon the earth?'

CHURCH SIGNS

REAL SIGNS FROM CHURCH NOTICEBOARDS

Free Trip to heaven. Details Inside!

Searching for a new look? Have your faith lifted here!

Have trouble sleeping? We have sermons – come hear one!

God so loved the world that he did not send a committee.

Come in and pray today. Beat the Christmas rush!

When down in the mouth, remember Jonah. He came out alright.

Fight truth decay – study the Bible daily.

How will you spend eternity – Smoking or Nonsmoking?

Dusty Bibles lead to Dirty Lives.

It is unlikely there'll be a reduction in the wages of sin.

Do not wait for the hearse to take you to church.

If you're headed in the wrong direction, God allows U-turns.

If you don't like the way you were born, try being born again.

Looking at the way some people live, they ought to obtain eternal fire insurance soon.

Forbidden fruit creates many jams.

In the dark? Follow the Son.

Running low on faith? Stop in for a fill-up.

If you can't sleep, don't count sheep – talk to the Shepherd.

BLESSING

Count your blessings instead of your crosses,

Count your gains instead of your losses,

Count your joys instead of your woes,

Count your friends instead of your foes.

Count your courage instead of your fears,

Count your laughs instead of your tears.

Count your full years instead of your lean,

Count your kind deeds instead of your mean.

Count your health instead of your wealth,

Count on God instead of yourself.

Irish Blessing

ACKNOWLEDGMENTS

With grateful thanks to:

Christian Classics Ethereal Library
Christian Road Safety Association
Christian Surfers of Australia
Christian Vegetarian Association
Christians in Science (www.cis.org.uk)
Christiananswers.net
Churchgeeks.com
David Chapman
DAWN Europe
Easton's Bible Dictionary
Gideons International
Holy Trinity Brompton
Kondansha Encyclopedia of Japan
Mark Wilson
Matthew Slick (Christian Apologetics and Research Ministry,
www.carm.org)
Open Doors
Stephen M Miller & Robert V Huber
Stephen Tomkins
The Book of Common Prayer and Administration of the Sacraments
The Jewish Encylopaedia
The Nobel Foundation
The Porvoo Churches
The Society of Friends
Westminster Abbey
Wholesomewords.com
William Hooper
William Landles

TEXT ACKNOWLEDGMENTS